Into the Mind of Infinity

By

Joe Livingston

PREFACE

I never planned to write *Into the Mind of Infinity*. It just sort of happened.

I'm not a scientist, so having an engineering background would probably be a significant reason for not drifting towards cosmology and the sciences.

But something resonated— call it intuition, premonition or just a hunch. As a result of this happening, my intellect steered me towards this unlikely topic and Thesis of the Cosmos.

When something "happens," which is undeniable, everything seems to click into place.

When I awoke that morning, that "click" moved into gear.

I heard in my mind, "Into the Mind of Infinity."

The sentence repeated and then again until I felt a hand guiding my typing and forcing me to write it down.

During my engineering profession (I am now retired), I was a qualified trainer and instructor in different engineering disciplines and theology subjects.

I loved teaching and demonstrating "how things work." Maybe curiosity pushed me in the direction of the sciences.

Intuition took control.

The eventual result of my exploratory typing was the completion of this book – about a year later. This book (Theosophy) will change your mindset about the cosmos and evolution and should appeal to laypersons, scientists, and academics alike.

Please take your time whilst reading my book, for it is an expose and combination of my scientific theories with some common sense thrown in. Lurking silently between the pages of this Theosophy, there is an intricate feeling of "Beyond Time." If you sense this, then you truly are bonded with The Mind Of Infinity.

Above all else, enjoy the book.

Scientists are already "clicking on to my theories," and varying critiques help the reader to understand them.

Please remember to send feedback via my email address joelivingston1967@gmail.com

With most sincere gratitude and best wishes to all who will read *Into the Mind of Infinity*.

One of the main reasons for my book is to try and bring souls to God by drawing atheists in the direction of the Eternal Creator.

"The Stars are Silent Writings of the Heavens"

Joe Livingston,
Author

FOREWORD

Joe's book is an expose on the complexities of the Cosmos and the inherent difficulties of bringing Science and Religion together. However, Joe–an engineer by profession–has very cleverly weaved together these differing strands of Religion and Science. A book that will challenge entrenched ideas and which is a living testament to Joe's faith in God. This faith helped to guide him in areas where he needed to trust the Holy Spirit more than his own skillset.

John Smith, Scientist (BSC, C, CHEM)

Table of Contents

CHAPTER 1

Always is

"Always was, always is and always will be!"

"Can you repeat that, please?"

"Always was, always is and always will be."

I'm confused already, don't know about you!

(Cause, Conception and Effect)

That explosive moment of conception.

It is a minute and unseen moment that irradiates light towards a perfect structure – similar to a microscopic globule of ink falling from a fountain pen onto a sheet of blotting paper.

The blob of ink is almost unseen to the human eye, until it starts to spread out on the blotting paper!

The ink then becomes rapidly visible to the human eye spreading out inexorably, forming a much larger imprint on the blotting paper.

The universes, the galaxies and the stars –the planets all in orbit, moving serenely within the blackness of outer space. The meteors, shooting stars and comets gliding in unseen symmetry.

The Hubble telescope brings into sharp focus the milky way and unseen galaxies.

Now the scientists are talking about black holes which suck stars into the core of their vast black density.

The moons of the various planets in our own solar system orbit freely in un-ending and varying orbital paths.

Our own moon seems to sit motionless in the evening sky, with the man in the moon smiling as usual.

Relentless disastrous weather patterns here on earth seem to be increasing.

Plagues and earthquakes are all too frequent.

Where are we in all of this?

Slap bang in the middle of it! Wondering, looking and thinking: "Where, when and how?"

What's it all about, Alfie?

Have we ever wondered why the planets in our own solar system don't collide?

Do we ever look at the intricacy of the human body and wonder?

What caused the supposed big bang? Is it linked to conception?

Quantum Physics, what? Look at the physics of the human body!

$E=MC2$.....is it relative?

If we had to take a journey into the mind of an infinite system of regenerating cells and explosive electrons, would we find any cohesion or symmetry?

Anything that has mass and occupies a volume of space can be looked upon as the building blocks of matter.

This type of detectable matter is called Baryonic matter.

Another area of matter, in this case, cosmic rays, can be seen as particles from outer space.

These particles, when they arrive at Earth collide with the Nuclei of atoms in the upper atmosphere, creating more particles, mainly pions.

The charged pions can swiftly *deca*, emitting particles called muons.

Unlike muons they do not interact strongly with matter and can travel through the atmosphere to *penetrate* below ground.

The rate of muons arriving at the surface of the earth is such that about one per second passes through a volume the size of a person's head.

Does this demonstrate that only the more robust muons can survive?

Even at this moment the physics of cosmic rays are still being analysed, leading to a study of a potential link between cosmic rays and *cloud formation*.

Cosmic rays are, in fact, charged particles that bombard the earth's atmosphere.

In 1929, the astronomer Edwin Hubble measured the velocities of a large selection of galaxies. He discovered that almost all galaxies are moving away from earth instead of coming towards it.

This suggests that a point of origin is drawing these galaxies back to their original source.

Scientists have also discovered the galaxies that are farthest away from the earth are the ones moving the *fastest*.

After talking about the physics of outer space, let's become even more intimate and look at the physics of conception in the womb.

We will look at the analogy of the human sperm's journey towards the female egg and its connecting pattern with time and space.

CHAPTER 2

Sperm Cells

Let us look at the amazing journey of human sperm (spermatozoa) that eventually blasts through the receptacle of a female egg (ovum) in the womb.

A sperm cell uses its flagellum – commonly known as a tail – to propel itself towards the female oocyte or egg.

It only needs 2×10-18 watts of power to propel it.

The hydrolysis of a single ATP molecule produces 10-19 joules of energy, so cellular motion requires very little energy expenditure.

Let us assume the speed of a sperm cell of 336 body lengths per second – that is the average of a salmon and whale speeds. Multiplying this number by the length of a sperm yields 18,000 ums or 18.5mms.

This is two or three orders of magnitude (100-1000 times) faster than the numbers cited in a recent study essay.

Sperm swimming at this speed would cover their "seven-inch journey" to the ovum (180mm) in under ten seconds.

The analogy of the galaxies moving towards their origin and the spermatozoa movement rate is very interesting.

Is there a reasonable hypothesis that all matter in the universes and galaxies in relation to the unique matter of the spermatozoa are not only moving towards the source of conception but also at great velocity?

Is there a suggestion here of some form of connection between the origin and movement of galaxies and the origin of human life?

Spermatozoa know exactly where they are going to the origin of human creation. It's a tough journey, and only the strongest sperm get to their ultimate goal of fertilization and conception.

At the moment of ejaculation, does the spermatozoa have some form of inherent knowledge of the importance of human life and survival?

It certainly seems that way.

Each small task of everyday life and sexuality is part of the total harmony of the universe.

Nothing comes from nothing.

CHAPTER 3

Cause and Effect

Everything that exists has something that caused it.

There is nothing in our world that came from nothing.

The *first* cause must have no beginning. That is, nothing caused it to exist because the first cause is eternal.

Let us look at the eloquent words of St Thomas Aquinas:

The first and more manifest way is the argument from motion. It is certain, and evident to our senses, that in the world, some things are in motion.

Now whatever is in motion is put in motion by another, for nothing can be in motion except it is in potentiality to that towards which it is in motion; whereas a thing moves inasmuch as it is in the act. For motion is nothing else than the reduction of something from potentiality to actuality. But nothing can be reduced from potentiality to actuality, except by something in a state of actuality.

Thus that which is actually hot, as fire, makes wood, which is potentially hot, to be actually hot, and thereby moves and changes it. Now it is not possible that the same thing should be at once in actuality and potentiality in the same respect, but only in different respects. A momentary change in the amount of energy - in a point within space.

It is, therefore, impossible that, in the same respect and in the same way, a thing should be both mover and moved, i.e. that it should move itself.

Therefore, whatever is in motion must be put in motion by another. If that by which it is put in motion be itself put in motion, then this also must need be put in motion by another, and that by another again.

But this cannot go on to infinity, because then there would be no first mover and, consequently, no other mover; seeing that subsequent movers move only inasmuch as they are put in motion by the first mover; as the staff moves only because it is put in motion by the hand. Therefore, it is necessary to arrive at a first mover, put in motion by no other. And this everyone understands to be God.

The second way is from the nature of the efficient cause. In the world of sense, we find there is an order of efficient causes. There is no case known (neither is it, indeed, possible) in which a thing is found to be the efficient cause of itself; for so it would be prior to itself, which is impossible.

Now in efficient causes, it is not possible to go on to infinity because in all efficient causes following in order, the first is the cause of the intermediate cause, and the intermediate is the cause of the ultimate cause, whether the intermediate cause be several or only one.

Now to take away the cause is to take away the effect. Therefore, if there is no first cause among efficient causes, there will be no ultimate, or any, intermediate cause. But if in efficient causes it is possible to go on to infinity, there will be no first efficient cause, neither will there be an ultimate effect, nor any intermediate efficient causes; all of which is plainly false. Therefore, it is necessary to admit a first efficient cause, to which everyone gives the name of God.

The third way is taken from possibility and necessity and

runs thus. We find in nature things that are possible to be and not to be since they are found to be generated and to corrupt, and consequently, they are possible to be and not to be. But it is impossible for these always to exist, for that which is possible not to be at some time is not.

Therefore, if everything is possible not to be, then at one time, there could have been nothing in existence. Now, if this were true, even now, there would be nothing in existence because that which does not exist only begins to exist by something already existing.

Therefore, if at one time nothing was in existence, it would have been impossible for anything to have begun to exist; and thus, even now, nothing would be in existence - which is absurd. Therefore, not all beings are merely possible, but there must exist something the existence of which is necessary. But every necessary thing either has its necessity caused by another or not.

Now it is impossible to go on to infinity in necessary things that have their necessity caused by another, as has been already proved in regard to efficient causes. Therefore, we cannot but postulate the existence of some being having of itself its own necessity, and not receiving it from another, but rather causing in others their necessity. This all men speak of as God.

The fourth way is taken from the gradation to be found in things. Among beings, there are some more and some less good, true, noble and the like.

But "more" and "less" are predicated on different things, according as they resemble in their different ways something which is the maximum, as a thing is said to be hotter according as it more nearly resembles that which is hottest; so that there is something which is truest, something best, something noblest and, consequently, something which is uttermost being. For those things that are greatest in truth are greatest in being, as it is written in Metaph. ii.

Now the maximum in any genus is the cause of all in that genus; just as fire, which is the maximum heat, is the cause of all hot things. Therefore, there must also be something which is to all beings the cause of their being, goodness, and every other perfection. And this we call God.

The fifth way is taken from the governance of the world. We see that things that lack intelligence, such as natural bodies, act for an end, and this is evident from their acting always, or nearly always, in the same way, so as to obtain the best result.

Hence it is plain that not fortuitously, but designedly, do they achieve their end. Now whatever lacks intelligence cannot move towards an end, unless it is directed by some being endowed with knowledge and intelligence; as the arrow is shot to its mark by the archer. Therefore, some intelligent being exists by whom all natural things are directed to their end. And this being we call God.

Five ways to prove that God exists - Aquinas.

Aquinas sets about the arguments fairly comprehensively. In the next chapter, we will look at Infinity.

CHAPTER 4

Infinity
What is Infinity?
Cosmological infinities

Another type of infinity arises in gravitation theory and cosmology. Einstein's theory of general relativity suggests that an expanding universe (as we observe ours to be) started at a time in the finite past when its density was infinite — this is what scientists call the Big Bang.

Einstein's theory also predicts that if you fell into a black hole, and there are many black holes in our galaxy, and nearby, you would encounter an infinite density at the centre. These infinities, if they do exist, would be actual infinities.

People's attitudes to these infinities differ. Cosmologists who come from particle physics and are interested in what string theory has to say about the beginning of the universe would tend to the view that these infinities are not real, that they are just an artifact of the unfinished character of our theory.

There are others. Roger Penrose is one, for example, who thinks that the initial infinity at the beginning of the universe plays a very important role in the structure of physics. But even if these infinities are an artifact, the density still becomes stupefyingly high - 1096 times bigger than that of water. For all practical purposes, that's so high that we need a description of the effects of quantum theory on the character of space, time, and gravity to understand what goes on there.

Something very odd can happen if we assume that our universe will eventually stop expanding and contract back to another infinity, a big crunch.

That big crunch could be non-simultaneous because some parts of the universe, where there are galaxies and so on, are denser than others.

The places that are denser will run into their future infinities before the low-density regions.

If we were in a bit of the universe that had a greatly delayed future infinity, or even none at all, then we could look back to see the end of the universe happening in other places — we would see something infinite. You might see evidence of space and time coming to an end elsewhere.

But it is hard to predict exactly what you will see if an actual infinity arises somewhere. The way our universe is set up at the moment, there is a curious defense mechanism. A simple interpretation of things suggests that there is an infinite density occurring at the centre of every black hole, which is just like the infinity at the end of the universe.

But a black hole creates a horizon around this phenomenon. Not even light can escape from its vicinity. So we are insulated. We cannot see what goes on at those places where the density looks as though it is going to be infinite. And neither can the infinity influence us.

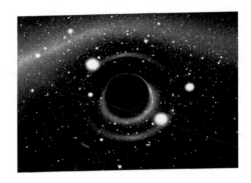

These horizons protect us from the consequences of places where the density might be infinite and they stop us seeing what goes on there unless, of course, we are inside a black hole.

Another question is whether our universe is spatially finite or infinite. I think we can never know. It could be finite but of a size that is arbitrarily large. But to many people, the idea of a finite universe immediately raises the question of what is beyond. There is no beyond — the universe is everything there is.

To understand this, let us think of two-dimensional universes because they are easier to envisage. If we pick up a sheet of A4 paper, we see that it has an edge, so how could it be that a finite universe doesn't have an edge? But the point is that the piece of paper is *flat*.

If we think of a closed two-dimensional surface that's curved – like the surface of a sphere – then the area of the sphere is finite – you only need a finite amount of paint to paint it. But if you walk around on it, unlike with the flat piece of paper, you never encounter an edge.

So curved spaces can be finite but have no boundary or edge. Einstein-space is curved.

To understand an expanding two-dimensional universe, let us first think of the infinite case in which the universe looks the same on average wherever you go. Then wherever you stand and look around you, it looks as though the universe is expanding away from you at the centre because every place is like the centre.

For a finite spherical universe, imagine the sphere as the balloon with the galaxies marked on the surface. When you start to inflate it, the galaxies start to recede from one another.

Wherever you stand on the surface of the balloon, you would see all those other galaxies expanding away from you as the rubber expands.

The centre of the expansion is not on the surface; it is in another dimension - in this case, the third dimension. So our three-dimensional universe, if it is finite and positively curved, behaves as though it is the three-dimensional surface of an imaginary four-dimensional ball.

(see diagram)

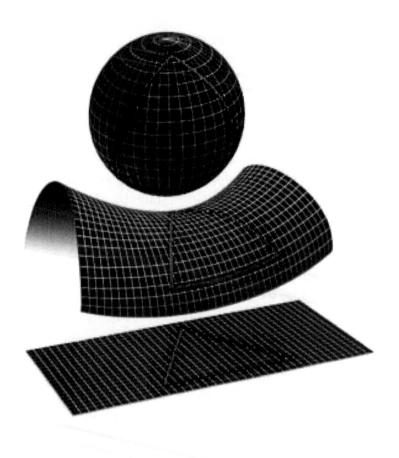

The sphere has positive curvature, the saddle has negative curvature, and the flat plane has zero curvature. The triangles are formed by drawing the shortest lines between pairs of points.

Where the sum of the angles exceeds (is less than) 180 degrees, the surface has positive (negative) curvature. When it equals 180 degrees, the surface is flat, with zero curvature.

Einstein told us that the geometry of space is determined by the density of material in it. Rather like a rubber trampoline

- if you put material on the trampoline, it deforms the curvature. If there is a lot of material in the space, it causes a huge depression, and the space closes up.

So a high-density universe requires a spherical geometry and it will have a finite volume. But if you have relatively little material present to deform space, you get a negatively curved space shaped like a saddle or a potato crisp. Such a negatively curved space can continue to be stretched and expand forever.

A low-density universe, if it has a simple geometry, will have an infinite size and volume. But if it has a more exotic topology, like a torus, it could also have a finite volume.

One of the mysteries about Einstein's equations is that they tell you how you can work out the geometry from the distribution of matter, but his equations have nothing to say about the topology of the universe. Maybe a deeper theory of quantum gravity will have something to say about that.

With kind permission of John D Barrow, Professor of Mathematics at Cambridge University and Overseer of e-magazine PLUS

Hopefully, the search for enlightenment will enhance the hunt for a deeper theory of quantum gravity.

There are different areas of infinity that should also be mentioned:

+ Mathematical Infinities.
+ Physical Infinities.

Infinity (often denoted by the symbol 8 or Unicode 8) represents something that is boundless or *endless*, or else something that is larger than any real or natural number.

Since the time of the ancient Greeks, the nature of infinity was the subject of many discussions among philosophers in the 17th century; with the introduction of the infinity symbol and the infinitesimal calculus, mathematicians (including *l'hopital* and Bernoulli regarded these as infinitely small quantities, but infinity continued to be associated with endless processes).

Infinity is endless and, therefore, cannot be reached. Thus, the expression "to infinity and beyond" would simply represent *limitless possibilities.*

CHAPTER 5

Mindset

Mindset in decision theory and general systems theory is a set of assumptions, methods or notations held by one or more people or groups of people.

A mindset can also be seen as an incident of a person's worldview or philosophy of life.

Can a mindset alter belief and common sense?

Determination to prove a scientific theory can open the door to irrational conclusions.

What happens when a scientific theory is proven to be wrong? Normally in the scientific world, they go back to the drawing board until they come up with another theory!

How can you theorise about the magnificence of the galaxies and the universes? It's literally laden with black holes!

Nothing comes from nothing.....Intelligent design? Now there's a theory for you!

If scientists can theorise, can we laypersons theorise?

Of course, we can.

What does intelligent design mean?

Intelligent design is a pseudo–scientific argument for the existence of God presented by its proponents as evidence based on scientific theory about life's origins.

CHAPTER 6

Does Infinity Have a Mind?

I remember a close relative once saying to me, "I can't get my head around infinity. I just can't."

When we look at the very thought or idea of infinity, it can be very challenging, to say the least.

The notion of infinity goes against all rational thoughts.

As I said in the introduction of this book: "Always was, always is and always will be."

Can infinity be controlled in some way?

Is it rational to think that something that is endless can have a consciousness?

If infinity does not have a beginning or an ending, what can we relate that to?

Let us take, for example, the complexity of human cells.

The link between DNA and protein.

The molecular structure of one human cell is truly astonishing.

For all of the components of one single cell to actually form by chance is in the trillions to one.

Something else is at work.

The mathematical probability of being able to create just one cell is pointing towards trillions to one.

So, something else is at work.

Common sense tells us that some form of intelligent design is at work.

Is it a spiritual equation?

Seems to be.

The mathematical probability of the human formation of an individual cell is blown into orbit when we just look at the story of the discovery and mind-blowing complexity of DNA and its fabulous formation.

CHAPTER 7

DNA

How was DNA first discovered, and who discovered it?

It is a common misconception that James Watson and Francis Crick discovered DNA in the 1950s. In reality, DNA was discovered decades before. It was by following the work of the pioneers before them that James and Francis were able to come to their ground-breaking conclusion about the structure of DNA in 1953.

The story of the discovery of DNA begins in the 1800s with the molecule of life.

The molecule now known as DNA was first identified in the 1860s by a Swiss chemist named Johann Friedrich Miescher.

Johann set out to research the key components of white blood cells, part of our body's immune system. The main source of these cells was pus-coated bandages collected from a nearby medical clinic.

Johann carried out experiments using salt solutions to understand more about what makes up white blood cells. He noticed that, when he added acid to a solution of the cells, a substance separated from the solution.

This substance then dissolved again when an alkali was added. When investigating this substance, he realised that it had unexpected properties different from those of the other proteins he was familiar with. Johann called this mysterious substance "nuclein" because he believed it had come from the cell nucleus.

Unbeknown to him, Johann had discovered the molecular basis of all life – DNA. He then set about finding ways to extract it in its pure form.

Johann was convinced of the importance of nuclein and came very close to uncovering its elusive role, despite the simple tools and methods available to him.

However, he lacked the skills to communicate and promote what he had found to the wider scientific community. Ever the perfectionist, he hesitated for long periods of time between experiments before he published his results in 1874. Before then, he primarily discussed his findings in private letters to his friends.

As a result, it was many decades before Johann Friedrich Miescher's discovery was fully appreciated by the scientific community.

For many years, scientists continued to believe that proteins were the molecules that held all of our genetic material. They believed that nuclein simply wasn't complex enough to contain all of the information needed to make up a genome.

Surely, one type of molecule could not account for all the variation seen within species. The four building blocks of DNA.

Albrecht Kossel was a German biochemist who made great progress in understanding the basic building blocks of nuclein.

In 1881 Albrecht identified nuclein as a nucleic acid and provided its present chemical name, deoxyribonucleic acid (DNA). He also isolated the five nucleotide bases that are the building blocks of DNA and RNA: adenine (a), cytosine (b), guanine (c), thymine (d) and uracil (e).

This work was rewarded in 1910 when he received the

Nobel Prize in Physiology or Medicine.

The chromosome theory of inheritance:

In the early 1900s, the work of Gregor Mendel was rediscovered, and his ideas about inheritance began to be properly appreciated. As a result, a flood of research began to try and prove or disprove his theories of how physical characteristics are inherited from one generation to the next.

In the middle of the nineteenth century, Walther Flemming, an anatomist from Germany, discovered a fibrous structure within the nucleus of cells. He named this structure 'chromatin' but what he had actually discovered is what we now know as chromosomes.

By observing this chromatin, Walther correctly worked out how chromosomes separate during cell division, also known as mitosis.

The chromosome theory of inheritance was developed primarily by Walter Sutton and Theodor Boveri.

They first presented the idea that the genetic material passed down from parent to child is within the chromosomes. Their work helped explain the inheritance patterns that Gregor Mendel had observed over a century before.

Interestingly, Walter Sutton and Theodor Boveri were actually working independently during the early 1900s. Walter studied grasshopper chromosomes, while Theodor studied roundworm embryos.

However, their work came together in a perfect union, along with the findings of a few other scientists, to form the chromosome theory of inheritance.

Walter Sutton and Theodor Boveri worked independently

to come up with the chromosome theory of inheritance.

Building on Walther Flemming's findings with chromatin, German embryologist Theodor Boveri provided the first evidence that the chromosomes within egg and sperm cells are linked to inherited characteristics.

From his studies of the roundworm embryo, he also worked out that the number of chromosomes is lower in egg and sperm cells compared to other body cells.

American graduate Walter Sutton expanded on Theodor's observation through his work with the grasshopper. He found it was possible to distinguish individual chromosomes undergoing meiosis in the testes of the grasshopper and, through this, he correctly identified the sex chromosome.

In the closing statement of his 1902 paper, he summed up the chromosomal theory of inheritance based on these principles:

- Chromosomes contain the genetic material.

- Chromosomes are passed along from parent to offspring.
- Chromosomes are found in pairs in the nucleus of most cells (during meiosis, these pairs separate to form daughter cells).
- During the formation of sperm and eggs cells in men and women, respectively, chromosomes separate.
- Each parent contributes one set of chromosomes to its offspring.

(Ref- dna structure.com)

All this points back to my theory about the relationship between expanding galaxies and the velocity comparison of male spermatozoa.

The complexity of chromosomes, being able to separate during formation, contributing to each parent - male and female being responsible for conception, points to the proof that all human existence is derived from only male and female origins and not the multitude of false genders that are forced upon the human race at this present time.

CHAPTER 8

DNA MOLECULE

(Ref dna – structure.com)

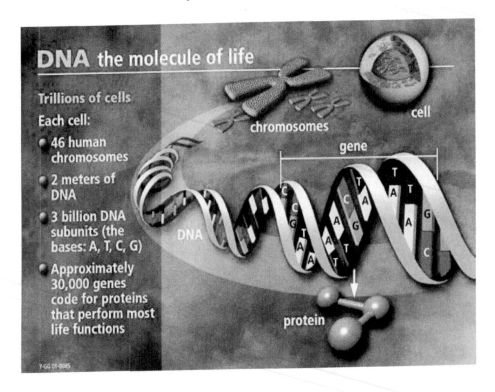

CHAPTER 9

Can Eternal Love be Seen Under a Microscope?

As I said earlier, trillions to one that all of this can happen by chance. Look at the statistics: 46 human chromosomes, three billion DNA subunits. All of this is in each cell.

Can all of this be achieved by human mathematics? Don't think so!

Maybe the missing link that scientists keep looking for is LOVE.

Let us assume that love created the galaxies and the universes, the stars, the planets, the comets and shooting stars.

If love created all of these, maybe it is not unreasonable to ask that if each particle within the whole of the galaxies was crushed into a powder what would remain?

It makes sense to suggest or theorise, as scientists do, that the only remaining element would be love.
But how do we find love under the microscope?

There is a real question.

If God is love and SPIRIT too, then the visible aspect of Divine Love would not be apparent under the microscope. We do know that God is love, so how do we define it?

Is love a separate entity from our lives, or is it really a part or *particle* of us?

Therefore, love could simply be within us, because God is love.

Every *particle* of love must come from a Creator. It makes further good sense to assume that if scientists ever find that elusive missing link, it will probably shock them to realise that the atomic composition of love cannot really be defined in theory.

How can scientists quantify a feeling or emotion which is part of the very fabric and substance of all human life?

Love is not just a feeling or emotion, it's a choice to will the good of the other. We can examine love through other people's actions and emotional behaviour. The microscope of our discernment tells us what love really is. It is not a mathematical equation. Love permeates the whole of creation, because *love Created love*.

How can we measure that?

The loving soul resonates with that measurement, fulfilling the eternal quest for the origin of life.

Providing the prime examples of dual cohesion and a peaceful existence.

CHAPTER 10

Splitting the Atom

When the universe is in harmony, life is peaceful.

If a situation or destructive force alters the free-flowing supernatural bonding of the galaxies there is, first of all, disruption, and secondly, a massive imbalance occurs, destroying the equilibrium.

One such destructive force happened at Los Alamos in 1945.

On July 16, 1945, the world's first atomic bomb was detonated 200 miles south of Los Alamos at Trinity Site on the Alamogordo Bombing Range. Under the project leadership of General Leslie R. Groves and staff direction of J. Robert Oppenheimer, scientists at the laboratory had successfully weaponized the atom.

Reference: lanl.gov/history/atomicbomb/trinity.shtml

J Robert Oppenheimer, the project leader, quoted some words from an ancient transcript.

"Witnessing the explosion," he said: "A few people cried, most were silent." Then he said, *"Now I have become death the destroyer of worlds."*

"I suppose we all thought that in one way or another."

You can actually sense the fear and tension in these famous words from Oppenheimer.

Within a matter of months, the very first atomic bomb was dropped on Hiroshima in Japan, obliterating that city and killing 146,000 on August 6, and another 80,000 in Nagasaki on August 9.

When the natural path of atomic structure is split, it can cause massive destruction and death.

The universe is made up of intricate galaxies and universes. They are kept in place by an unseen force that is responsible for free-flowing movement and amazing solar cohesion.

What would happen if the *unseen force* removed all spiritually supernatural guidance?

The atomic explosion gives us a good idea.

Destruction on a massive scale comes to mind.

To clarify further, there are three main sub-atomic particles - Protons, Electrons and Neutrons (PEN)

Only Electrons and Protons are charged. All atoms want to have full electron shells or orbitals for stability. They achieve this by either sharing electrons (covalent bonds) or loss or gain electrons.

Metal atoms generally lose electrons to form positive ions.

For example Na + , or – Non-metal atoms gain electrons to form negative ions

Therefore, they come together to form compounds like

NaCl (salt) with very strong electronic bonds – with very high melting points – it takes tremendous amounts of energy to break these bonds.

CHAPTER 11

When We See a Chair,
Is it Actually a Chair?

The structural elements of matter are the atoms, which consist of a nucleus and the atomic shell. The properties of solids are essentially determined by the electron shell structure. According to the Bohr model of an atom, the electrons occupy specific orbitals, the configuration of which, i.e., the number of electrons and their spatial arrangement, follows the laws of quantum mechanics.

The most important electrons for the properties of a solid are the electrons in the outermost orbital, because they determine the interaction with other atoms.

The dominant principle of atomic interaction is the tendency of an atom to have its outermost shell filled with eight electrons, i.e., the noble gas configuration. This simple principle is the foundation of chemical bonding. If an atom already has a complete outer shell with eight electrons, like the noble gases, then its tendency to interact with other atoms, i.e., for *chemical bonding* or even for *solidification,* is very small. Helium has to be cooled to 0.1 K to make the interaction forces between the atoms sufficiently large compared to the thermal vibrations *to generate a solid.*

All elements which do not have a noble gas configuration have the tendency (since associated with an energy gain) to accept, to donate, or share the outermost electrons, also referred to as valence electrons, when in contact with other atoms. *From these principles we obtain the fundamental types of atomic bonding.*

The structural elements of matter are the atoms, which consist of a nucleus and the atomic shell. The properties of solids are essentially determined by the electron shell structure. According to the Bohr model of an atom, the electrons occupy specific orbitals, the configuration of which – i.e., number of electrons and their spatial arrangement - follows the laws of quantum mechanics.

The most important electrons for the properties of a solid are the electrons in the *outermost orbital*, because they determine the interaction with other atoms. The dominant principle of atomic interaction is the tendency of an atom to have its outermost shell filled with eight electrons, i.e. the noble gas configuration.

This simple principle is the foundation of chemical bonding. If an atom already has a complete outer shell with eight electrons, like the noble gases, then its tendency to interact with other atoms, i.e., for chemical bonding or even for solidification, is very small.

Helium must be cooled to 0.1 K to make the interaction forces between the atoms sufficiently large compared to thermal vibrations to generate a solid. All elements which do not have a noble gas configuration have the tendency (since associated with an energy gain) to accept, to donate, or to share the outermost electrons, also referred to as valence electrons, when in contact with other atoms. *From these principles, we obtain the fundamental types of atomic*

Ref *https://link.springer.com/chapter10.1007/978-3-662-09291-0 3*

We can see by carefully studying the explanation above that everything we look at in our everyday lives is simply atomic matter.

Everything in the world is made from about 100 different chemical elements that join together in different ways to form all the solids, liquids and gases we see around us.

Once again, it is very obvious that the probability of all these elements just HAPPENING to come together to form the very seats that we sit on is highly unlikely.

All roads lead to Origin.

Is common sense common?

The outer structure of a chair is designed by the furniture maker.

Do the furniture designers realise that the materials they use to construct the chair, including wood, upholstery material, glue varnish and paint, have already been atomically designed by an unseen force?

It's amazing, isn't it?

The formation of all elements in the world point back to origin and intelligent design.

Throughout this book, I have tried to show a logical sequence and common-sense approach to mankind's origin.

The magnificent structure of the whole universe can sometimes seem to be awe-inspiring, and yet there are, as I call them, "The Searchers." Always trying to figure out magnificence.

It's a tall order.

Even Einstein said: *"The more I study science, the more I believe in God."*

And a further quote: *"The only way to overcome the problem of an Intelligent Universe is by Faith."*

Here we have one of the foremost scientists of yesteryear telling us to tread carefully in the direction and meaning of origin.

It was purported that Einstein was an agnostic.

And yet even in his agnosticism, he still marvelled at the complexity of the galaxies.

It is said that when he finally had the eureka moment in solving the theory of relativity, he knew deep in his heart that an unseen helping hand was at work.

I'm not a scientist, but when intuition merges with common sense, the sense of a higher level of reasoning develops, culminating in a deeper acceptance of the blinding moment of discovery that can often elude us.

We shouldn't try to search too deeply. Acceptance and reasoning are great attributes to attain.

Sometimes when we surrender our frailties, things begin to happen.

It's almost as if the *Intelligent Designer* decides to step in and reward our complete helplessness.

CHAPTER 12

Nature

Nature is the physical world collectively including plants, animals, the landscape and other features and products of the earth, as opposed to humans or human creations.

When the world at large refers to the word *mother nature,* there is a difference in meaning.

Mother Nature is a Greco-Roman personification of nature that focuses on life-giving and nurturing aspects of nature by embodying it in the form of the mother.

Images of a woman representing mother earth and mother nature are meant to be supposedly timeless.

Karl Marx referred to nature, saying, "It is absolutely impossible to transcend the laws of nature. What can change in historically different circumstances is only the form in which these laws expose themselves."

http://www.brainyquote.com/quotes/karl_marx_401619

Here Marx is saying that it is impossible to go beyond the limits of nature, although the future history of these laws can alter in form under different circumstances.

Historically different circumstances can mean a lot of different things.

Does it also mean that *time* can eventually alter proven events?

Brings us back to the theory of relativity.

Let us look at General Relativity

Special Relativity (1905)

CHAPTER 13

The Theory of Relativity

General Relativity: (1915)

Suppose that you are moving toward something that is moving toward you. If you measure its speed, it will seem to be moving faster than if you were not moving. Now suppose you are moving away from something that is moving toward you. If you measure its speed again, it will seem to be moving more slowly. This is the idea of "relative speed" - the speed of the object relative to you.

Before Albert Einstein, scientists were trying to measure the "relative speed" of light. They were doing this by measuring the speed of starlight reaching the Earth. They expected that if the Earth was moving toward a star, the light from that star should seem faster than if the Earth was moving away from that star.

However, they noticed that no matter who performed the experiments, where the experiments were performed, or what star light was used, the measured speed of light in a *vacuum* was always the same.

Einstein said this happens because there is something unexpected about length and duration, or how long something lasts.

He thought that, as Earth moves through space, all measurable durations change very slightly. Any clock used to measure a duration will be wrong by exactly the right amount so that the speed of light remains the same.

Imagining a *"light clock"* allows us to better understand this remarkable fact for the case of a single light wave.

Also, Einstein said that as Earth moves through space, all measurable lengths change (ever so slightly). Any device measuring length will give a length off by exactly the right amount so that the speed of light remains the same.

The most difficult thing to understand is that events that appear to be simultaneous in one frame may not be simultaneous in another. This has many effects that are not easy to perceive or understand. Since the length of an object is the distance from head to tail at one simultaneous moment, it follows that if two observers disagree about what events are simultaneous, then this will affect (sometimes dramatically) their measurements of the length of objects.

Furthermore, if a line of clocks appears synchronized to a stationary observer and appears to be out of sync to that same observer after accelerating to a certain velocity, then it follows that during the acceleration, the clocks ran at different speeds. Some may even have run backwards. This line of reasoning leads to *general relativity*.

Other scientists before Einstein had written about light seeming to go at the same speed no matter how it was observed. What made Einstein's theory so revolutionary is that it considers the measurement of the speed of light to be constant by definition, in other words, it is a *law of nature*. This has the remarkable implications that speed-related measurements, length and duration, change in order to accommodate this.

Simplified: The central idea of General Relativity is that *Space and Time* are two aspects of spacetime.

Here is a brief description of *Special Relativity*, a theory in physics that was developed and explained by Albert Einstein in 1905.

It applies to all physical phenomena, as long as gravitation is not significant.

Special Relativity applies to "Flat Spacetime" or the Minkowski Principle. *Ref; Simple WikiPedia .org*

I hope that while you are reading this story of *Into the Mind of Infinity*, you will see the many correlations between scientists (unconsciously) writing about the existence of intelligent design in *one form or another*.

When I started writing this book, I had no idea of what the format would be, even the content, although I had done various bits of research, it now seems I was being guided by an unseen hand and mind.

Still on the subject of nature, let us now look at some examples of life on our most amazing planet.

CHAPTER 14

Metamorphosis

Metamorphosis is a biological process by which an animal or insect physically and sometimes abruptly develops after birth or hatching into a different body structure through cell growth and differentiation.

Some insects, fish, amphibians, molluscs and crustaceans also undergo metamorphosis, which is often accompanied by a change in nutrition and behaviour.

FIRST EXAMPLE: the caterpillar.

As I watched the time-lapse footage of a caterpillar changing into a moth, I was completely amazed.

We see science fiction movies about the mutation of humans into another species, but this is fiction (at the moment!)

Whilst watching the present-day reality of the metamorphosis of the caterpillar, I have to say I was completely awe-struck. I marvelled at this complete change of one insect into another.

What on earth can cause this miracle of change?

Or do we have to look at the other possibility, of the inherent involvement of a special set of circumstances?

The transformation of the caterpillar into a moth takes

approximately five to twenty-one days, according to research from 2008, adult Manduca sexta is able to retain *behaviour learned as a caterpillar.* Another caterpillar, the ornate moth caterpillar, is able to carry toxins that it acquires from its diet through metamorphosis and into adulthood, where the toxins still serve for protection against predators.

Is the mind of the universal creation involved in the learned behaviour of the caterpillar?

Look at the toxins that the caterpillar is able to carry as a defence mechanism against predators!

This is real evidence of both a paternal and universal code of ethics towards mere insects.

www.quora.com/do-moths-come-from-caterpillars

SECOND EXAMPLE: Frogs and Toads.

Again, I can go back to my childhood and well remember locating darting tadpoles in some countryside ponds. It always amazed me that these tadpoles turned into frogs!

With frogs and toads, the external gills of the newly-hatched tadpole are covered with a gill sac after a few days, and lungs are quickly formed. Front legs are formed under the gill sac, and hind legs are visible a few days later. Following that, there is usually a longer stage during which the tadpole lives off a vegetarian diet. Tadpoles use a relatively long, *spiral*-shaped gut to digest that diet. (DNA - Spiral Helix)

Rapid changes in the body can then be observed as the

lifestyle of the frog changes completely.

The *spiral*-shaped mouth with horny tooth ridges is reabsorbed together with the *spiral* gut. The animal develops a big jaw, and its gills disappear along with its gill sac. Eyes and legs grow quickly, a tongue is formed, and all this is accompanied by associated changes in the neural networks (development of stereoscopic vision and loss of lateral line system etc.).

All this can happen in about a day!

So it is truly a metamorphosis?

It is not until a few days later that the tail is reabsorbed due to the higher thyroxin concentrations required for tail resorption.

Even a tadpole has neural (nervous system) networks!

Let us analyse the anatomy of the tadpole in a more studious way.

The tadpole has a *spiral*-shaped gut.

During the 1990s, scientists discovered the constellation Draco, a remarkably shaped galaxy.

The galaxy resembled a tadpole and is now Tadpole Galaxy.

The massive trail of stars gives off the appearance of a tadpole.

The trail of the *tail* is 280,000 light-years long.

The *head* of the tadpole is in the area of the dwarf galaxy that's nearest to the two poachers – that's stars lingering in the victim galaxy which formed the tail.

Here are some images of the tadpole galaxies.

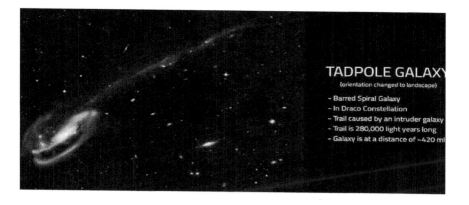

TADPOLE GALAXY
(orientation changed to landscape)

- Barred Spiral Galaxy
- In Draco Constellation
- Trail caused by an intruder galaxy
- Trail is 280,000 light years long
- Galaxy is at a distance of ~420 ml

The spiral-shaped gut of the tadpole led me to the magnificent tadpole-shaped galaxies.

The spiral helix of the DNA structure points to spiral-shaped galaxies.

The Tadpole Galaxy leads me back to origin and intelligent design, just like the birth of the tadpole.

With just two examples of true metamorphosis, I would like to think it is quite evident that there are definite links back to the fact of *supernatural* origin and intelligence.

49

Did all the evidence already shown just happen by chance?

Can mathematics recreate all the evidence already shown?

CHAPTER 15

The Birth of Creation

For a few years now, scientists have been searching for a reason and an account for the birth of all creation.

"Like the Fire that Transforms Everything into Itself."

What?

Yes, exactly right, transforming birth.

It's a creation that transforms everything back into itself!

Impossible!

Not for intelligent design.

If we look at the scientific theories of creationism, this will give us a better understanding of the debate.

Creation science, or scientific creationism, is a pseudoscience, a form of creationism presented without obvious Biblical language but with the claim that special creation and flood geology based on the Genesis creation narrative in the Book of Genesis have validity as science. Creationists also claim it disproves or re-explains a variety of scientific theories of geology, cosmology, biological evolution, archaeology, history, and linguistics.

However, the overwhelming consensus of the scientific community is that creation science fails to qualify as scientific because it lacks empirical support, supplies no tentative hypotheses, and resolves to describe natural history in terms of scientifically untestable supernatural causes.

Courts, most often in the United States where the question has been asked in the context of teaching the subject in public schools, have consistently ruled since the 1980s, that creation science is a religious view rather than a scientific one.

Historians, philosophers of science, and skeptics describe creation science as a pseudoscientific attempt to map the Bible into scientific facts. Professional biologists have criticized creation science for being unscholarly. *Ref Wikipedia.org*

If creationism mentions the fact of the special creation and flood geology of the (Genesis narrative) in the Book of Genesis, it shows a certain validity as a science.

So here we have a connection between Science and the Bible according to the Creationists. (I tread very carefully here, because mainstream science can differ in many ways from pseudo-science).

If we look at the narrative of Genesis in the Bible, it should open up more clues about the birth of creation.

Genesis 1: 1-31

Genesis 1:1 In the beginning God created the heavens and the earth.

This opening verse of the Bible establishes seven key truths upon which the rest of the Bible is based.

First, God exists. The essential first step in pleasing God is recognizing His existence (Heb 11: 6).

Second, God existed <u>before</u> there was a universe and will exist after the universe perishes (Heb 1: 10-12).

Third, God is the main character in the Bible. He is the subject of the first verb in the Bible (in fact, He is the subject of more verbs than any other character) and performs a wider variety of activities than any other being in the Bible.

Fourth, as Creator, God has done what no human being could ever do; in its active form, the Hebrew verb *bara'*, meaning "to create," never has a human subject. Thus, *bara'* signifies a work that is uniquely God's.

Fifth, God is mysterious; though the Hebrew word for God is plural, the verb form of which "God" is the subject is singular. This is perhaps a subtle allusion to God's Trinitarian nature: He is three divine persons in one divine essence.

Sixth, God is the Creator of heaven and earth. He doesn't just modify pre-existing matter but calls matter into being out of nothing (Ps 33: 6,9; Heb 11: 3).

Seventh, God is not dependent on the universe, but the universe is totally dependent on God (Heb 1: 3).

If we dissect Genesis 1 even further. At the very beginning of Genesis 1 v 2, there is a tremendous clue to origin itself: "Now the earth was a FORMLESS VOID ...."

Let us look at the word "formless."

Definition: Without a clear or definite shape or structure.

He doesn't just modify pre-existing matter but calls matter into being out of nothing (Ps 33: 6,9; Heb 11)

The next part of the debate is this:

Atheists will say, "Don't believe in God. Therefore, I don't believe in the Bible."

Fair comment, but my reply to the atheists is: Do you realise that the Bible is the most popular book in the world?

53

Do you realise that the words written in the Bible are spiritually enhanced? Do you realise that the Bible is a well-verified written account from over 2000 years ago?

Again, the arguments are plain to see. Sometimes it takes the *GRACE* of faith and belief to cement the *Eureka Moment*. Throughout the remainder of Genesis, it is very clearly stated about how the formless became formed.

The Scientific View of Creation

The scientific view of creation and the Big Bang is a common question among people as to why are things the way they are. How *was* our world created?

There are many different theories from a variety of views. In this paper, I will discuss the scientific view of the Creation Theory. The theory that I will be discussing is the Big Bang. This is currently the theory of creation accepted by most scientists as the explanation of the beginning of the universe.

The Big Bang Theory suggests that the universe was once extremely compact, dense and hot. Some uncommon event, a cosmic explosion, caused the big bang, occurring about 10 billion to 20 billion years ago, and the universe has since been expanding and cooling.

(www.bartleby.com/essay/scientific-view-of-creation-and-the-big-pkckw6ly)

What I would like to ask during your decision-making is. What created the Cosmic Explosion and the Big Bang?

CHAPTER 16

Making Form out of The Formless

The previous chapter mentioned the Big Bang, so we are progressively moving forward with the story to highlight situations of importance as they arise in a methodical way.

The simplest models in which the Big Bang was caused by quantum fluctuations. That scenario had very little chance of happening, but it took place instantly, in our perspective, due to the absence of time before the Universe.

Bigbangwiki-pedia.org/wiki/big_bang

Quantum Fluctuations

In quantum physics, a quantum fluctuation (or vacuum state fluctuation or vacuum fluctuation) is the temporary change in the amount of energy in a point in space, as explained in Werner Heisenberg's uncertainty principle. This allows the creation of particle-antiparticle pairs of virtual particles. *ewwikipedia.org/wiki/quantum_fluctuation*

The wording, "Due to the absence of time," quoted in the Big Bang statement above, is very interesting. Does this suggest everlasting and *timeless?*

Does it suggest that infinity is linked to some form of causation, e.g., in reference – a momentary *change in the amount of energy in a point in space?*

Everything is pointing to cause and effect, which I demonstrated earlier in my book.

Nothing comes from nothing.

If we analyse the momentary change aspect in reference to the Big Bang, we see a correlation.

Let us break this down methodically.

Earlier in this book, I spoke about the first atomic bomb detonation at Los Alamos (a *momentary change* in history).

The whole sequence leading up to the chain reaction within the bomb was set up by *human beings* (they were the causation) of that devastating explosion.

The horror of the atom bomb was described aptly by Robert Oppenheimer.

Quantum fluctuation theory allows for the creation of particle, and anti particle pairs of virtual particles (*This allows the creation of particle-and anti-particle pairs of- virtual particles*)

Does this sound familiar in regards to an atomic chain reaction?

Just to be clear.

Let us repeat the sentence above:

"This allows the creation of particle and anti-particle pairs of- virtual particles." It's a perfect description of a chain reaction of varying atoms that may well cause destruction, not formation of the universes as the scientists contend.

That is why the theory of quantum fluctuations seems to be flawed.

Intelligent design lovingly creates.

We only need to marvel at the wonderful variety of galaxies, universes and star systems to realise that any implied particle chaos (fluctuations) is exactly that.

There is no symmetry.

A Creator (Intelligent Designer) of all good things *visible* and *invisible* seems to be a reasonably sound answer to the scientific problems that continually arise.

CHAPTER 17

Design and Creation

Design in Nature

Sixth Senses

Our five senses cannot detect everything. The world is full of information beyond our reach, but many animals have "sixth senses"- super senses that enable them to experience other dimensions of our world. These bonus senses help these creatures survive and thrive in their habitats.

Amazing Design in Cells

If our genes and cells arose randomly through competition for supremacy, then how can we explain so many wonderful processes where cells are programmed to sacrifice themselves for the good of the whole, especially during development?

Divinely Designed Defenses

The defense mechanisms of just about every group in the animal kingdom could provide us with a lifetime of enjoyable study. It appears that these abilities were genetically present in the original creatures but activated after Adam sinned when God cursed the creation.

Horse Leg Bones

At first glance, horse legs appear to be poorly designed.

Taking a closer look at the equine leg bone, however, scientists have discovered unexpected features that give it amazing strength and may inspire new engineering ideas.

https://answersingenesis.org/evidence-for-creation/design-in-nature/beauty-undeniable-witness/

Creation in Nature

All around us, we see glorious nature in all its beauty.

+ When we can witness the raw power of 60 ft waves in the world's oceans.

+ When we watch the biological miracle of a baby being born.

+ When we see the complexity of the anatomy of the human body.

+ When we see the mountains, valleys, and rivers.

+ When we see the galaxies and stars.

+ When we see the glory of a perfect sunrise and sunset.

CHAPTER 18

Living Organism

Throughout this book thesis, I have put forward some theories about the Origin of Life and surrounding galaxies.

Each step of the way, I have tried to demonstrate various theories about the relationship between "The Big Bang" and its opponent, "Intelligent Design."

From the first chapter (always is) describing Einstein's "Theory of Relativity," we do learn that everything in the galaxies is indeed relative in composition.

This very chapter, called "Living Organism," attempts to describe how organisms relate to what has already been described in previous chapters, from sperm cells and "infinity" through to "mindset" and the Mind of Infinity.

DNA led us through to molecule, love and "splitting the atom," and so on.

Within the evidence provided so far, there always seems to be a correlation and connection to something far larger regarding our very existence.

I am not trying to communicate a preference as to the very creation of the galaxies; what I have been trying to evaluate and show is the fundamental fact that something else is at work.

Many eminent scientists have tried to explain the birth of our Universes and Galaxies and of our very existence.

What about this theory – did Jesus Christ really exist?

Four eminent Evangelists attest to this.

Did Jesus Christ understand or relate to intelligent design? - I think He did.

Just listen to some of his discourses contained throughout the Holy Bible. I digress a little here, but I'm trying to bring forth more evidence as to the Creation of Everything described in Genesis.

Let us look at the connection between organisms and bacteria.

Unlike in multicellular organisms, increases in cell size (cell growth) and reproduction by cell division are tightly linked in unicellular organisms.

Bacteria grow to a fixed size and then reproduce through binary fission, a form of asexual reproduction.

Ref Image- Quora

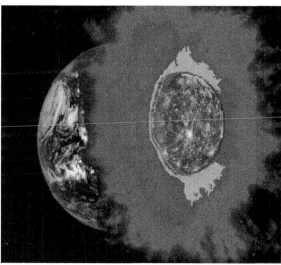

Scientists on board the International Space Station (ISS) have discovered living bacteria clinging to the orbital facility's external surface, according to a prominent Russian cosmonaut.

Anton Shkaplerov, who will return to the ISS next month (2017) says cotton swabs wiped over the exterior of the station's Russian segment revealed an unidentified lifeform that has already been sent back to Earth for scientific analysis.

"It turns out that somehow these swabs reveal bacteria that were absent during the launch of the ISS module," Shkaplerov told Russian news agency TASS.

"That is, they have come from outer space and settled along the external surface. They are being studied so far, and it seems that they pose no danger."

According to Shkaplerov, the samples were taken during extravehicular activity, probing obscure areas around the ISS exterior and places where fuel waste accumulates from discharge of the station's engines.

What makes the discovery potentially exciting is that, at present, we've been given no explanation for just how the organisms got there – nor what exactly they are.

Characteristics of Living Organisms

Living organisms have the following characteristics in common:

- Movement - they can move and change their position.

- Reproduction – they can make more of the same kind of organism as themselves.

- Sensitivity– they can detect or sense stimuli and respond to them.

- Growth - they can permanently increase their size or dry mass by increasing the number or size of their cells.

- Respiration – they can create chemical reactions that break down nutrient molecules in living cells to release energy.

- Excretion – they can excrete toxic materials, waste products of metabolism, and excess substances (note that excretion is not the same as egestion).

- Nutrition - they can take in and absorb nutrients such as organic substances and mineral ions. These nutrients contain the raw materials or energy needed for growth and tissue repair.

The first letter of each of these characteristics makes up the acronym MRS GREN. This is a good way of remembering them.

Living organisms can also control their internal conditions, such as their temperature or water content.

Let's analyse the characteristics of "Living Organisms."

1. They have movement: Can they change position movement in space? Who or What is causing the movement?

2. Reproduction: They can make more of the same kind of organism as themselves! Is intelligent design at work here? This shows a very clear path towards the creation factor, similar to sperm cell production.
3. Sensitivity: (tenderness) they can sense stimuli and respond …..feelings?

4. Growth: They can permanently increase their size or DRY MASS by increasing the number or size of their cells! Also, increasing the size of their Cells points to origin and new birth.
5. Respiration: They can create chemical reactions that break down nutrient molecules in living cells to release ENERGY.

CREATE CHEMICAL REACTIONS! A release of ENERGY! This suggests FORMATION.

6. Excretion: They can excrete toxic materials, waste products of metabolism. It suggests cleansing in the very source of organisms.
7. Nutrition: They can take in and absorb nutrients. For a successful lifespan, every organism needs nutrients. In the Theory of Intelligent Design, sustainability is a prerequisite for survival. Creation

designates the absorption of all the organisms needed to sustain symmetry, cohesion and biological growth.

The seven descriptions that have been explained are already inherent in all matter.

There is no finite explanation for all of the explanations that are being presented.

The more we look at the internal structures of universal matter that are both visible and INVISIBLE, the more I am inclined to lean towards a very complex and loving mind that is responsible for creation.
Ref Quora

CHAPTER 19

My Theory as to *The Order Of Creation*

Molecular structure was formed when the BAPTISM (which symbolises purification and REGENERATION) of the Holy Spirit (Engulfed the formless void) creating life. (The Alpha and The Omega).

Is there a reason for creation?

Yes.

Because it pleased intelligent design to do so. The Creator was already there – in the formless void.

The Formation: (always will be)
When a formless structure is baptised (regeneration – or renewal of a biological system), there is a spiritual engulfing by the Holy Spirit providing power and energy, just like the fire that transforms everything into itself.

"My Spirit" engulfed time and matter – in a spiritual baptism. (Not an explosion or a big bang). To engulf means to Sweep Over something so as to surround or Cover It completely. What ensued was an engulfing of the nothingness and void - baptising and creating a spiritual formation of molecular structures – which all came into visible reality in the stunning birth of all galaxies and star systems. All of these galaxies, universes and star systems were linked together similar to a theoretical bicycle chain (polymer) in motion (oscillating, with inbuilt metamorphism), built up chiefly or completely from a large number of similar galactic units, bonded together.

Prior to the baptism or engulfing by the Holy Spirit, the bicycle chain was already within the formless void, unseen and unrecognised. The engulfing of the nothingness put the final double LINK of the bicycle chain into a connecting and secured place, forming the continuous movement and expansion of the universes that we see today.

It was the sealing (link) of the Holy Spirit.
The creation of the cosmos was a form of supernatural fission (splitting into galaxies).

The Order of Creation

1. Always is (beyond infinity) Alpha and Omega.

2. Baptism of the Holy Spirit (Energy released and revealed) through the infinite reasoning of the Creator.
3. Mass is formed through the power (released energy) of the Holy Spirit.
4. This mass is visibly transformed, giving birth to the planets, universes, galaxies and (nebulas).
5. Man created to adorn the symmetry.

Who can know the mind of Intellectual Design?

My theory is born through the information that I have already provided in this book.

Many times, I have thought about infinity.

Did it just happen? No. Nothing comes from Nothing.

There has to be a cause, and my *order* above is a simple theoretical answer to a complex argument.

CHAPTER 20

Cosmological Order

A system of beliefs that seeks to describe or explain the origin and structure of the universe. A cosmology attempt to establish an order, harmonious framework that integrates time, space, the planets, stars, and other celestial phenomena.

This cosmological order is remarkably similar to the divine order in the sense that it is a framework that integrates time and space, the planets, stars, and other celestial phenomena. But, unfortunately, it is an attempt to establish these cosmological realities.

This cosmological framework was so complex that it prompted Einstein to add a constant to his Theory of Relativity.

Here is a description of that constant.

Cosmological constant is a term reluctantly added by Albert Einstein to his equations of general relativity in order to obtain a solution to the equations that described a static universe, as he believed it to be at the time.

The constant has the effect of a repulsive force that acts against the gravitational attraction of matter in the universe.

Even Einstein could see the complexities of a universe that were constantly changing.

CHAPTER 21

Nebula *(Noun)

In the previous chapter, I mentioned a Nebula. Here is information to continue the scientific flow of this thesis.

A nebula is a cloud of gas and dust (dust to dust) in outer space, visible in the night sky, either as an indistinct bright patch or as a dark silhouette against other luminous matter.

When a lot of mass accumulates within a nebula, the gravitational attraction increases, and the nebula collapses to form a star. This does not happen with a galaxy, meaning that the galaxy as a whole does not collapse to give birth to a star.

Galaxies exist in different shapes and sizes and also with varying brightness. They are thus classified based on these factors. Generally, they are classified into three broad categories: (a) spiral (b) elliptical (c) irregular.

Nebulae are also generally classified on the basis of their structure. Their classifications are, however, different than those of galaxies. Mainly nebulae are categorised into the following four types: (a) emission nebulae (b) HII regions (c) supernova remnants (d) dark nebulae.

Although it may seem ironic, in addition to nebulae being formed at star birth, they can also be formed when a star implodes. A galaxy, however, is not formed during such an implosion. Galaxies are also found in space in forms of clusters or groups. No such pattern has yet been observed for nebulae.

Galaxies and nebulae are different features of the vast

universe in which we live. The main thing to note is that they differ greatly in their size, and while galaxies possess many stars, a nebula is just the beginning or end of one star. Nebula is a cloud of interstellar dust, while a galaxy is a huge collection of stars.

Nebula cause star formation. Nebula is present within a galaxy. Galaxy cannot be present within a nebula. Nebulae are classified into emission, HII region, supernova remnant, and dark.

Galaxies are classified into spiral, elliptical, and irregular. Galaxies live longer than nebulae.

The life of several stars is connected to life of a galaxy, while the life of only one star is associated with a nebula. Galaxies can be found in clusters in space.

Another difference to note is that galaxies generally have a longer life span than that of a nebulae. This is because a nebula is just one thing in a vast galaxy that can constitute up to more than millions of stars.

The life of a galaxy is thus connected with the lives of all the stars within it. This also means that if a galaxy implodes, millions or billions of stars will die with it, but a nebula only results in one star's death.
Ref http://www.differencebetween.net/science/difference-between-nebula-and-galaxy/#ixzz6QO2rmI

Within the mind of infinity all of these complexities are simple and workable, because the designer knows his own work.
If another person tries to understand a design drawing, for instance, it usually requires the actual designer to explain the finer points of the design itself.

Image of Nebula
Ref – Image Wikipedia

CHAPTER 22

What is the Eternal Soul?

A nebula has a dust component. That dust is almost like the soul of the nebula, sometimes unseen – but it is there.

Let us look at the soul in more depth.

From a scientific perspective:

Traditionally, science has dismissed the soul as an object of human belief or reduced it to a psychological concept that shapes our cognition of the observable natural world. The terms "life" and "death" are thus nothing more than the common concepts of "biological life" and "biological death."

From an intelligent design perspective:

Virtually every Christian church admits to a belief in the rejoining of an incorruptible physical body with the eternal soul at the time of the resurrection. This is known as the "resurrection of the body" doctrine and is included in many affirmations of faith. For example, from the "Apostles' Creed."

The primeval and eternal One begets by emanation nous (intelligence); and from nous, in turn, springs psyche (soul), which is the image of nous, but distinct from it. Matter is a still later emanation.

The soul is the subject of human consciousness and freedom; soul and body together form one unique human nature. Each human soul is individual and immortal, immediately Created by God.

The human person, created in the image of God, is a being at once corporeal and spiritual. The biblical account

71

expresses this reality in symbolic language when it affirms that "then the Lord God formed man of dust (nebula) from the ground and breathed into his nostrils the breath of life (Baptism of the Holy Spirit – *No 2 in the Order of Creation*) and man became a living being. Man, whole and entire, is, therefore, willed - see *(No 5 in Order Of Creation)* by God.

In Sacred Scripture, the term "soul" often refers to human *life* or the entire human *person*. But "soul" also refers to the innermost aspect of man, that which is of greatest value in him, that by which he is most especially in God's image: "Soul" signifies the *spiritual principle* in man.

The human body shares in the dignity of "the image of God:" it is a human body precisely because it is animated by a spiritual soul, and it is the whole human person that is intended to become, in the body of Christ, a temple of the Spirit.

Man, though made of body and soul, is a unity. Through his very bodily condition, he sums up in himself the elements of the material world. Through him, they are thus brought to their highest perfection and can raise their voice in praise freely given to the Creator. For this reason, man may not despise his bodily life. Rather he is obliged to regard his body as good and to hold it in honour since God has created it and will raise it up on the last day.

The unity of soul and body is so profound that one has to consider the soul to be the "form" of the body. That is; because of its spiritual soul, the body made of matter becomes a living, human body; spirit and matter, in man, are not two natures united, but rather their union forms a single nature.

The Church teaches that every spiritual soul is created immediately by God - it is not "produced" by the parents - and also that it is immortal. It does not perish when it separates from the body at death, and it will be reunited with the body at the final Resurrection.

Sometimes the soul is distinguished from the spirit. St Paul, for instance, prays that God may sanctify his people "wholly" with "spirit and soul and body," kept sound and blameless at the Lord's coming. The Church teaches that this distinction does not introduce a duality into the Soul. "Spirit" signifies that from creation, man is ordered to a supernatural end and that his Soul can gratuitously be raised beyond all it deserves to communion with God.

The spiritual tradition of the Church also emphasizes the *heart*, in the biblical sense of the depths of one's being, where the person decides for or against God. (CCC 362). *Ref School of Apologetics CA*

To continue with the flow, it is interesting that two scientists have developed a quantum theory proving the existence of the human soul.

A pair of world-renowned quantum scientists say they can prove the existence of the Soul.

American Dr Stuart Hameroff and British physicist Sir Roger Penrose developed a quantum theory of consciousness asserting that our Souls are contained inside structures called microtubules which live within our brain cells.

Their idea stems from the notion of the brain as a biological computer, "with 100 billion neurons and their axonal firings and synaptic connections acting as information networks."

Dr Hameroff, Professor Emeritus at the Departments of Anesthesiology and Psychology and Director of the Centre of Consciousness Studies at the University of Arizona, and Sir Roger have been working on the theory since 1996.

They argue that our experience of consciousness is the result of quantum gravity effects inside these microtubules - a process they call orchestrated objective reduction (Orch-OR).

In a near-death experience, the microtubules lose their quantum state, but the information within them is not destroyed. Or, in layman's terms, the Soul does not die but returns to the universe.

Dr Hameroff explained the theory at length in the Morgan Freeman-narrated documentary Through the Wormhole, which was recently aired in the US by the Science Channel.

The quantum soul theory is now trending worldwide, thanks to stories published recently by The Huffington Post and the Daily Mail, which have generated thousands of readers' comments and social media shares.

"Let's say the heart stops beating, the blood stops flowing, the microtubules lose their quantum state," Dr Hameroff said.

"The quantum information within the microtubules is not destroyed; it can't be destroyed, it just distributes and dissipates to the universe at large.

"If the patient is resuscitated, revived, this quantum information can go back into the microtubules, and the patient says, 'I had a near-death experience'."

In the event of the patient's death, it was "possible that this quantum information can exist outside the body indefinitely - as a soul." *Ref News.com.au*

Throughout the writing of this book, I have been fairly cautious to always try to debate from both sides of the argument regarding the existence of intelligent design.

Hopefully, I have managed to keep that balance. However, I apologise if my deliberations at times seem to sway gently towards my inherent beliefs.

What can I add about the existence of the human soul? I feel the explanation at the start of this chapter regarding intelligent design perspective is fairly sufficient to put over my side of the debate.

Just a thought to add further.

Isn't it interesting that the words we use in our everyday language can mention the soul, and sometimes people might not even realise this. Here are some examples:

The international distress signal SOS (Save our Souls).

"Let's get to the heart and soul of the matter."

"Look at that building; it has no soul."

"He was the life and soul of the party."

"Soul Mates."

Is the word soul ingrained into our language for a reason, or did it just happen?

I'll leave the logic of that decision up to you!

CHAPTER 23

Galaxy Types and Sizes

Galaxies come in three main types: ellipticals, spirals, and irregulars. A slightly more extensive description of galaxy types based on their appearance is given by the Hubble sequence. Since the Hubble sequence is entirely based upon visual morphological type, it may miss certain important characteristics of galaxies, such as star formation rate (in starburst galaxies) and activity in the core (in active galaxies).

As we can see, the complexity of space can sometimes overwhelm us. For example, if we look again at the structure of a nebula (shown previously), where is the location of the dust contained in a nebula? Is it on the outside or the inside of the nebula?

Nebulae are made of dust and gases, mostly hydrogen and helium.

The dust and gases in a nebula are very spread out, but gravity can slowly begin to pull together clumps of dust and gas. As these formations get larger and larger, their gravity gets stronger and stronger.

Complex? Let us continue by trying to unravel the nebula secrets, and the first port of call has to be gravity, which seems to be a formation of sorts.

Gravity was discovered by Isaac Newton, almost by accident. Isaac explored a dozen different subjects, including light, astronomy, mathematics, chemistry and physics.

When he tired of one subject, he switched to some other unsolved mystery of science.

For instance, scientists were puzzled by the fact that bodies on earth and bodies in the heavens appeared to follow different laws. Imagine a ball rolling across a perfectly smooth and level table. It rolls forward at a constant speed in a straight line. It only slows because of air resistance and the friction between it and the table.

The moon, like a ball on a flat and perfectly smooth table, keeps moving year after year without slowing. However, the moon does not travel in a straight line. Instead, it circles the earth.

Why does the moon not travel in a straight line?

Isaac Newton remembered the force of the wind. Although invisible, it turned his windmill. The force of the storm had uprooted trees. He concluded that a force acts upon the moon to bend its straight-line path into a closed orbit.

What was the unknown force?

One day an apple fell from the tree overhead and banged onto Isaac's worktable in the orchard. He picked up the apple. As he held it, he noticed the moon, which had risen in the east.

Could it be, Isaac asked, that the moon and the apple are both subject to the same force of gravity? Isaac proved that gravity acts on both the apple and the moon.

He showed that earth's gravity extends far out into space and controls the moon in its orbit.

Isaac Newton returned to Cambridge, where he taught mathematics. Working off and on for the next 20 years, he proved that all objects attract each other according to a simple equation. The sun, moon, planets, even apples and grains of sand are all subject to the law of gravity.

The law of gravity became Isaac Newton's best-known and most important discovery. Isaac warned against using it to view the universe as only some machine like a great clock.

He said, *"Gravity explains the motions of the planets, but it cannot explain who set the planets in motion. God governs all things and knows all that is or can be done."*
www.brainyquote.com/quotes/isaac_newton_737903

As the years passed, people came to understand the importance of his many discoveries. Isaac received many honours. In 1705, Queen Anne knighted him Sir Isaac Newton. It was the first knighthood for scientific discoveries rather than deeds on the battlefield or in government. When Isaac Newton died in 1727, the poor country boy from Woolsthorpe was buried in a plot reserved for a king.

Despite his fame as a scientist, the Bible and not nature had been Isaac Newton's greatest passion. He devoted more time to Scripture than to science.

He said, *"I have a fundamental belief in the Bible as the Word of God, written by those who were inspired. I study the Bible daily."*

Ref www.doesgodexist.org/novdec01/isaacnewtonandgods

Once again, we see a very powerful correlation between the workings and structure of the universes, in this case, a nebula.

Gravity pulls the gas and dust together.

As the formations of gas and dust get bigger and bigger, the gravitational force gets stronger!

It's like an unseen hand forming everything.

Let us look at Sir Isaac's comments again. "Gravity explains the motions of the planets, but it cannot explain who sets the planets in motion. God governs all things and knows "all that is or can be done."

If ever a simple sentence verified all that I have been saying in this book, then here it is.

Here we have an eminent scientist telling us not to get carried away with scientific calculations and theories, and to stick to the basics, look to intelligent design as the answer to ALL THAT IS or CAN BE DONE.

Is there a super answer to all this?

Everything in the cosmos is, for want of a better word, super. It truly is a super formation. (in the English language, we will say, "I had a super day"etc).

What if we take that word a step further and add natural? Is the cosmos natural or unnatural?

Certainly not unnatural.

Therefore, I would have to say it is natural.

So, if we add the two words together, we get supernatural!

A supernatural cosmos provides us with so many wonderful, complex, and visible signs of variety and multiplicity that it is almost impossible to try to fathom everything out.

Let us look at some more of this breathtaking evidence.

CHAPTER 24

Supernova

Interesting about the word <u>supernova</u>.

Let us now look at the meaning: A supernova (/ˌsuːpərˈnoʊvə/ plural: supernovae or supernovas, abbreviations: SN and SNe) is a powerful and luminous stellar explosion.

This transient astronomical event occurs during the last evolutionary stages of a massive star or when a white dwarf is triggered into runaway nuclear fusion.

The original object, called the progenitor, either collapses into a neutron star or a black hole or is completely destroyed. The peak optical luminosity of a supernova can be comparable to that of an entire galaxy before fading over several weeks or months.

Runaway Nuclear <u>Fusion</u>?

Does this suggest <u>formation</u> again?

Origin?

Supernova Image

Bright spot on the lower left is a type of supernova within its host Galaxy NGC 4526.
URL=http://en.wikipedia.org/wiki/Supernova by Nasa /esa,ccby3.0.https//commons.wikin

CHAPTER 25

Super Clusters

It's that word <u>super</u> again!

Before we isolate the superclusters, let us have a general look at the composition of galaxies.

Are galaxies similar in composition? Yes, according to some scientists.

However, spectral measurements of stars, dust clouds and galaxies tell us about the elemental composition of the portion that consists of normal matter.

Most Abundant Elements in The Milky Way Galaxy

This is a table of elements in the Milky Way (our galaxy) which is similar in composition to other galaxies in the universe.

Some galaxies occur alone or in pairs, but they are more often parts of larger associations known as groups, clusters, and superclusters.

Similar in composition strikes me as being part of an overall design.

Let us look at a diagram of the different types of galaxies to give you a better idea about the enormity of the cosmos.

Size (left) and distance (right) of a few well-known galaxies.
(*Image courtesy CosmoBrain, Reddit, Wikipedia*)

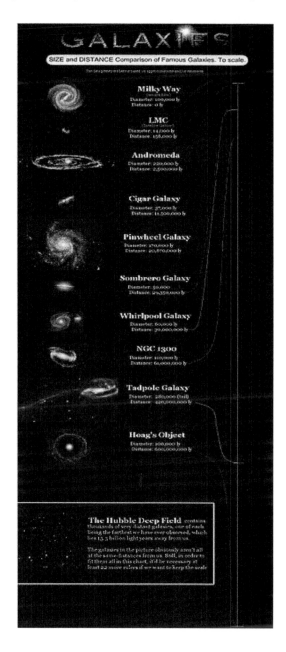

There are about 51 galaxies in our local grouping.

There are 100,000 in our local supercluster and an estimated one to two trillion in all the observable universe.

This data again shows us the complexities of the universes and, more importantly, the similarities in the formation of these wonderful heavenly bodies – which leads me to believe in the invisible link up described in the previous chapters regarding the Bicycle Chain theory.

Let us look at other areas of the Creative Mind and Intelligence within the vast domain of space.

What comes to my mind at this particular moment is a reading from the Bible: "For he it was who formed the mountains, Created the wind, reveals his MIND to man, makes both Dawn and Dark, and walks on the top of the heights of the World; the Lord God of Sabaoth is his name" *(Doxology - Amos 4 v 13).*

Methodically, we move on. Now let us analyse the invisible link up of the galaxies in more depth.

CHAPTER 26

Unseen Methodology

Some galaxies emit different colours.

If the average temperature of a galaxy is hot enough to emit a radiation towards the UV spectrum, the colour will be blue, violet or green. If the temperature is not hot, it will be towards the infrared, which is red, orange, yellow. Also, when a galaxy is closer to us, it appears blue, and if it is away from us, it appears red.

Based on my theory of connectivity, on the next page is a theological grid sketch of the Universal Flat Plane.

When studying this grid sketch, we must remember to take into consideration the invisible and inherent oscillation coupled with continual atomic curved (e.g. light can bend) metamorphosis that is contained within this flat plane grid example of the eternal cosmos.

(e.g. space-time around the sun is curved)

Einstein proved that his equations were correct. That during an eclipse, the position of the stars around the Sun moved ever so slightly - showing literally that space-time is curved.

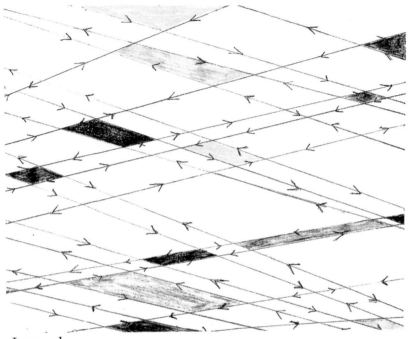

Legend:

Chevrons < represent Directional Curved Time and Mass.

Colour Code:

Blue, Violet and Green represent hot emission galaxies.

Red, Orange and Yellow represent cooler Emission Galaxies.

Of general interest:

Galaxies that are furthest away tend to be red in colour.

Galaxies that are nearer to us tend to be blue in colour.

Blank spaces in the grid represent multiple hidden galaxies.

I believe that the unseen connectivity of the universes could well be likened to a criss-cross pattern of flat space (see grid sketch on previous page).

Now that it is established that there is correlation and similarity between galaxies, we can now look at this question:

Does a galaxy emit sound?

Yes.

As soundwaves spread through the hot gas in galaxies and galaxy clusters – regions of greater pressure (soundwave peaks) tend to appear brighter in x-rays. Fainter regions (troughs) are dimmer.

Chandra X-ray telescope observations of the Perseus Cluster show roughly concentric ripples of brighter and fainter gas, which indicate sound waves.

Even the planets emit sound.

NASA has free download audio presenting the sounds emitting from the planets.

The <u>Voice of Earth</u> sounds like the dawn chorus of birds. The sounds from the Saturn Rings and Uranus Rings are similar. Jupiter, Neptune, and even one of the moons of Uranus called Miranda, all emit sound.

Astronomers in England have discovered a singing black hole in a distant cluster of galaxies. In the process of listening in, the team of astronomers not only heard the lowest sound waves from an object in the Universe ever detected by humans, but they also discovered an important clue about the formation of galaxy clusters, the largest structures in the cosmos.

Dr Andrew Fabian and his colleagues at the Institute of Astronomy in Cambridge, England, made their discovery using NASA's Chandra X-ray Observatory, an orbiting x-ray telescope that sees the universe in x-ray light, just as the Hubble Space Telescope sees it in visible light.

The black hole is situated in the centre of a galaxy amid a group of thousands of Galaxies collectively called the Perseus Cluster and located 250 million light years from

Earth (meaning it took the light from these galaxies 250 million years to reach us). The sound waves coming from it are in the form of a single note. *(NASA)*

We have now established the very real claim that sounds *do* emit from the galaxies.

Galaxies are similar in composition.

Again, (as I have done throughout this book) I am providing evidence of some sort of Design within the cosmos.

Why would sound be coming directly to us from the cosmos?

Dare I once again make a theoretical/spiritual suggestion?

As I said earlier in the book, a designer is the best person to ask about the theory behind his technical knowledge and design skills.

The designer knows everything about his conceptual blueprints.

If design complexities are inherent within the blueprint, there are always BOXED (go back to grid) notes to assist those who are studying the drawing.

These information bullets draw the engineering personnel to a quicker understanding of sometimes complex technical data contained within the blueprint.

Therefore, with this analogy of intelligent design, I will provide the readers of my book with another simple and obvious answer to the sounds being received from the cosmos.

Could it be that a SPECIAL Designer is showing us that his blueprint is there for all to see and hear?

It relates to a power beyond our understanding.

CHAPTER 27

Formless Power

Is it feasible if we link knowledge (knowing everything) to a formless void or vacuum, would there be an equation or (end result) basis for a Theory of Connectivity?

Millions of stars make up the Milky Way (what movement in these celestial paintings) suggest a formed guidance.

Let them see that the formations of the formed and the unformed are equal in theory.

Therefore, there is a constant at work - and it is nothingness.

Does nothingness (maybe even a vacuum) have physical or theoretical movement?

If so, where is the source of that movement?

My Heart and My Life is fixed knowledge within the formless structure and the nothingness of The Cosmos.

Therefore, if we can detect any form of pulsation (pulsating) is this a correlation fusion veering towards an Intelligent Higher Power comprising of a universal heart?

Not only was it very lasting about three seconds, but there were periodic peaks that were remarkably precise, emitting every fraction of a second - boom boom boom - *LIKE A HEARTBEAT.*

Does formless power have an equation?

Yes, I believe it does have a theory of being relative.

The constant of nothingness is relative to movement.

(Movement, is it visible?)

Non-visible power within a constant cosmological environment is evidence of a beating pulsating heart. Does formless power have an equation? Let us try to dissect this theory.

Yes, I believe it does. It is the theory of being relative, the constant of nothingness is relative to movement.

(Supernatural movement, is it visible?)

Non-visible power within a constant cosmological environment is evidence of a beating, pulsating heart (e.g. pulsars)

"Twinkle Twinkle, little star, how I wonder what you are?"

We will look at this in more detail soon.

What is my formula?

$$\text{Universal Constant} = \frac{\text{Nothingness X Power}}{\text{Infinity}}$$

The stars are everywhere in the night sky.

Let us have a look at some types of stars.

CHAPTER 28

Pulsars

NOTHINGNESS

This representation of nothingness is interesting in relation to my formula on the previous page.

A circle within a circle!

This is to let the discerning mind open up to different thought processes and meanings of certain symbols.

Pulsar

A pulsar (from pulse and -ar as in quasar) is a highly magnetized rotating neutron star that emits beams of electromagnetic radiation out of its magnetic poles. This radiation can be observed only when a beam of emission is pointing toward Earth (much like the way a lighthouse can be seen only when the light is pointed in the direction of an observer), and is responsible for the pulsed appearance of emission. Neutron stars are very dense and have short, regular rotational periods. *This produces a very precise interval between pulses* that ranges from milliseconds *to seconds* for an individual pulsar. Pulsars are one of the candidates for the source of ultra-high-energy cosmic rays (see also centrifugal mechanism of acceleration).

All human beings have a pulse. There is a very precise interval between pulses. This pulse emanates from the heart.

Is there a correlation here that a pulsar is actually *beating along the lines of a human heartbeat?*

Once again, we have a finger pointing directly back to creation and origin.

Intelligent design has, at its very core, a beating heart.

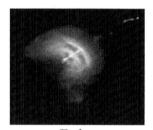

Pulsar

Ref Encyclopedia Britannica

CHAPTER 29

Star in the East

What could the 'Star in the East' be? One can claim that Matthew's Gospel describes a miracle.

(From: Mathew Chap 2: 7, 9; and Numbers 24:17.)

No star can do these things, nor can a comet, or Jupiter, or a supernova, or a conjunction of planets, or any other actual bright object in the night-time sky. words describe a miracle, something beyond the laws of physics. But Matthew chose his words carefully and wrote "star in the east" twice, which suggests that these words hold specific importance for his readers.

Can we find any other explanation, consistent with Matthew's words, that doesn't require that the laws of physics be violated, and that has something to do with astronomy? The answer, amazingly, is yes.

Astronomer Michael Molnar says that "in the east" is a literal translation of the Greek phrase *en te anatole*, which was a technical term used in Greek mathematical astrology 2,000 years ago. It described, very specifically, a planet that would rise above the eastern horizon just before the sun would appear. Then, just moments after the planet rises, it disappears in the bright glare of the sun in the morning sky. Except for a brief moment, no one can see this "star in the east."

We need a little bit of astronomy background here. In a human lifetime, virtually all the stars remain fixed in their places; the stars rise and set every night, but they do not move relative to each other. The stars in the Big Dipper appear year after year always in the same place.

But the planets, the sun and the moon wander through the fixed stars; in fact, the word "planet" comes from the Greek word for wandering star. Though the planets, sun and moon move along approximately the same path through the background stars, they travel at different speeds, so they often lap each other. When the sun catches up with a planet, we can't see the planet, but when the sun passes far enough beyond it, the planet reappears.

And now we need a little bit of astrology background. When the planet reappears again for the first time and rises in the morning sky just moments before the sun, for the first time in many months after having been hidden in the sun's glare for those many months, that moment is known to astrologers as a heliacal rising. A heliacal rising, that special first reappearance of a planet, is what *en te anatole* referred to in ancient Greek astrology.

In particular, the reappearance of a planet like Jupiter was thought by Greek astrologers to be symbolically significant for anyone born on that day.

Thus, the "star in the east" refers to an astronomical event with supposed astrological significance in the context of ancient Greek astrology.

CHAPTER 30

Polestar (North Star)

Moving on now, we look at the polestar, also called (Northern Hemisphere) North Star – the brightest star that appears nearest to either celestial pole at any particular time.

Owing to the procession of equinoxes, the position of each pole describes a small circle in the sky over a period of 25,772 years.

Each of a succession of stars has passed near enough to the north celestial pole – to serve as a polestar. At present the polestar is Polaris (a Ursa Minoris).

Thuban (a draconis) was closest to the North Pole about 2,700 BC, and the bright star Vega (a lyrae) will be the closest to the pole in 14,000 AD.

The location of the northern polestar has made it a convenient object for navigators to use in determining Latitude and north-south direction in the northern hemisphere. There is no bright star near the south celestial pole; the present southern polestar – Polaris Australis (also called Octantis) is only of the fifth magnitude and is barely visible to the naked eye.

As we look at this wonderful alignment of the North Star, is it not interesting that navigators can rely on this northern polestar for determining their latitude and north-south direction?

Once again, we have to look at this in more detail.

Why would there be a navigational constant in the sky?

Did it just HAPPEN that way?

Or would it be prudent to suggest that intelligent design prefers to give a little directional help to all these navigators?

CHAPTER 31

Neutron Star

A neutron star is a celestial object of very small radius (typically 30 kms) and very high density, composed predominantly of closely packed neutrons.

Neutron stars are thought to form by the gravitational collapse of the remnant of a massive star after a supernova explosion, provided that the star is insufficiently massive to produce a black hole.

Another type of neutron star is called a magnetar.

In a typical neutron star, the magnetic field is trillions of times that of the Earth's magnetic field. However, in a magnetar, the magnetic field is another 1000 times stronger.

There are two classes of non-quiet neutron stars – pulsars and magnetars.

So magnetars emit sound too! (Back to Origin) So magnetars emit sound too, which reveals a source of origin.

The magnetar also has a powerful magnetic field. (North and South Poles) relative to the theory of magnetism.

The Northern Polestar mentioned previously just happens to be relative to - the Northern and Southern Poles of a simple magnet. It is a directional constant and guide.

MAGNETISM: All substances exhibit some type of magnetism.

Ferromagnetism is responsible for most of the effects of magnetism encountered in everyday life, but there are actually several types of magnetism.

Paramagnetic substances, such as aluminium and oxygen, are weakly attracted to an applied magnetic field.

Diamagnetic substances such as copper and carbon are weakly repelled, while anti-ferromagnetic materials, such as chromium and spin glasses, have a more complex relationship with a magnetic field.

The strength of a magnetic field almost always decreases with distance, although the exact mathematical relationship between strength and distance varies. Different configurations of magnetic moments and electric currents – can result in complicated magnetic fields.

Magnets repel and attract other magnets and attract magnetic substances. Magnetic fields can be shown using field lines. Magnetism is induced in some materials when 99placed in a magnetic field.

Finding a Magnetic Field (see next page for diagram).

Field Lines around a Bar Magnet

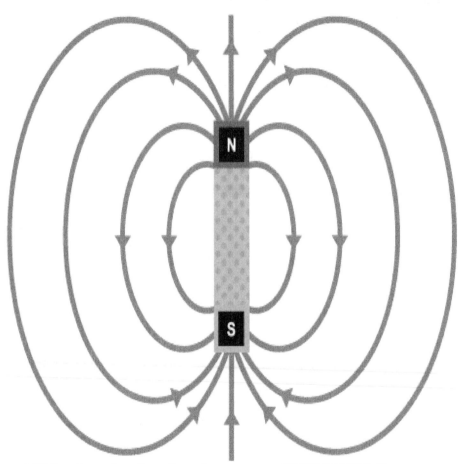

<u>NB</u> Look at the directional arrows or CHEVRONS (See my Diagram- <u>Flat Plain</u> Cosmos)

Ref: <u>lambdageeks.com/whatisthemagneticfieldaroundabarmagnet</u>

Moving from North to South (<u>Northern Pole</u> Star – Directional) - Study the magnetic lines going around the bar magnet (Origin) and returning to the original source.

My logic tells me that a simple flat bar magnet can show us

within its magnetic field a very powerful source of - (Return to sender!)

The oscillations I spoke about that are integral to the movement patterns in my grid sketch (shown by the chevrons) are very obvious in the diagram of the magnetic field surrounding the flat bar magnet.

All substances exhibit some form of magnetism.

Does this demonstrate the existence of a fairly comprehensive pattern of subatomic movement, which seems to go directionally towards some form of origin or original source? The magnetic directional patterns in all substances would therefore curve back to a very specific source.

A new study explains the phenomenon that sets the properties of stars and their orbiting planets.

Using simulations, researchers tracked wind material as it interacts with the ambient cloud.
They deduced that winds and radiation emitted by stars are responsible for significant energy transfer within molecular clouds, an impact enhanced by magnetic waves.

Ref – Nasa earthobservatory.nasa.gov/features/clouds

Therefore, we can see that all stars are within a galactic magnetic field, which has already been described previously, as pointing back to a powerful source of origin.

This chapter started with a description of a neutron star, but by a gentle directional nudge I came upon the theory of magnetism.

Was this intentional design, or was it a simple fluke or happening?

I will leave you to decide.

Let's look at some other stars now, including formations.

CHAPTER 32

The Sun

The sun is the closest star to Earth, about 93 million miles away. Our eyes are dazzled by it.

Our planet Earth is bathed in the sun's flow of radiation, washed by the winds of its outer atmosphere.

Atoms blow out from the sun's surface, bombarded by bursts (pulses) of x-rays and radio waves being emitted by it .

The sun is a ball of hydrogen and helium, whose diameter is roughly 100 times the size of the Earth

Image of Sun

Ref: www.shutterstock.com/search/sun

Scientists say that these huge flares from the surface of the sun could probably disrupt communications here on Earth - if they expand even further - without warning.

Whenever I study an image of the sun's surface, it always

reminds me of a *Burning Bush* fire.

Incredibly just today (after finishing the above sentence) I was reading the Daily Mail as of Friday July 17th 2020. Low and behold an image taken by a UK-built (spacecraft) called Solar Orbiter has taken incredible close-range photographs of our sun's surface.

These photographs show miniature flares across the surface of the sun, which look like "*Campfires*" that are millions of times smaller than the solar flares that are seen from Earth. (This is a direct and divine confirmation about what my theories are about).

In fact, during the recent bush fires in Australia, many TV images would show exactly what you see in the image of the sun presented in the previous page.

God appeared to Moses as a *Burning Bush* (Christianity and Judaism).

Is there a link back to origin in my *Burning Bush* theory?

If we dissect the sun's turbulent surface even further, most of the corona around the sun is held close by loops of magnetic field lines.

In x-rays, these magnetic field lines appear bright.

Every human being is a good conductor of electricity.

According to reputable sources including *The Journal Of Neuroscience,* the magnetic neuro-currents produced in your body are almost 5000 times weaker than your body's natural currents.
Ref: https://pubmed.ncbi.nlm.nih.gov/28710579

Therefore, it is conclusive that each human being is a walking magnetic field (intelligent design).

How many times during our earthly conversations have we

heard things like: "She has a magnetic personality," or "I was drawn to him like a magnet."

Does the subconscious mind interact with the magnetic field and induce these types of comments?

Within the previous pages regarding magnetism, it was proven that even within the theory of North and South Poles there is a leaning back towards origin and supernatural design.

Now we add a little more about my theory of magnetism and nudge forward with the methodology of proof.

Do the North and South curved patterns of magnetic movement (around the magnet) suggest an enveloping or (baptism) of the source material (magnet)?

Recheck my theory of "The Order of Creation."

This curved pattern of magnetic movement must be evident throughout the star system of the cosmos, showing us quite definitively that the galactic star systems point back to an enveloping of supernatural and grace-filled original Baptism.

It is interesting that the magnet (or any magnet) *draws* metal towards it.

(See below for a further extension of my theory of expanding matter and magnetic mass.)

The magnetic design source is forever drawing us through magnetic attraction to its surface.

Always is, always will be, beckoning us back to the supernatural, maternal and loving source of origin and intelligent design.

In a sense, the nothingness of the cosmos was a series of random oscillating lines of molecules encouraging envelopment. (Spiritual Baptism).

These oscillating molecular lines eventually collided through the inherent law of attraction contained within the material structures and their magnetic fields. These colliding forces then formed and extended into varying metamorphic lines, which is called matter.

This (now-formed) matter stretches into hyperspace in varying trajectories, re-colliding with other segments of expanding matter to become a magnetic mass.

A mass, which through structural metamorphosis and reasoning becomes a solid entity resulting in the birth of ever-changing galactic planes (both horizontal flat spacetime, vertical space time and axial and curved spacetime).

All this molecular activity is directly relative to the Polestar, a constant in the universal cosmos.

These fabulous universes of our cosmos are hosts to so many different types of stars. So moving on from the sun (our nearest star) let us now look at another one of the 13 main types of stars – called a Red Dwarf.

CHAPTER 33

Red Dwarf Star

A Red Dwarf Star is the smallest and coolest kind of star on the main sequence.

Red Dwarfs are by far the most common types of stars in the Milky Way, at least in the neighbourhood of the sun.

Individual Red Dwarfs cannot be easily observed from the Earth because of their low luminosity. Proximo Centauri, the nearest star to the sun, is a Red Dwarf – as are fifty of the sixty nearest stars.

The reason it is coloured red is because there are great chunks of the spectrum that are absorbed by molecules in the photosphere of the star. These molecules form at below 4000k temperature.

There is a tiny Red Dwarf star called TVLM, which has an amazingly powerful magnetic field.

Astronomers have also discovered an ultra-cool Dwarf Star. This star is called TVLM 513 – 465546. It is located just 35 light years from the Earth.

This Red Dwarf sits in the middle, between stars (which fuse Hydrogen), but Brown Dwarfs don't.

The lack of nuclear fusion makes the presence of the strong magnetic fields even more mysterious.

Magnetism in the sun comes from the movement of charged particles in its interior, similar to an electro-magnet where electric currents generate a magnetic field.

At the moment, it is unclear where its magnetic field

originates.

Once again, we have a clear indication that the unseen hand of intelligent design is at work, but also (bringing confusion to the scientists) *forming* the source of these powerful magnetic fields.

This is another explanation provided for a scientific mystery.

CHAPTER 34

Halo Stars

The Halo Stars is the name given to the ancient formation of stars which encircle the outer edge of the Milky Way.

A Galactic Halo (in ancient pagan - Halo symbolised Divinity) is an extended roughly spherical component of a Galaxy that extends beyond the main visible component.

Several distinct components of galaxies comprise of the Halo.

The distinction between the Halo and the main body of the galaxy is clearest in spiral galaxies where the spherical shape of the Halo contrasts with the Flat Disc (see my sketch of flat plane cosmos).

Only about one percent of a galaxy's stellar mass resides in its Halo.

Halo stars stand out because they formed before supernova explosions, which had scattered a large number of heavy elements into the galaxy. Therefore, Halo stars possess little iron.

Scientists have just found the biggest thing in the universe – a vast Mysterious Ring, five-billion light years across. It's so big that researchers have no idea why it exists, and it contradicts all current models of the universe. Another extraordinary find (Voyager) is that the realm of space is actually getting denser the further away from Earth we travel.

As previously demonstrated in the Red Dwarf chapter, again, we will methodically reveal the Divine Counter Claim of intelligent design regarding the Halo Stars.

1   Researchers have NO IDEA why this vast Halo exists.

2   They say it is mysterious (full of mystery).

3   It contradicts ALL current models of the universe.

Three very specific questions from the scientists regarding the vast ring, which they have no answer to.

Dare I be prudent once again and suggest a little theory about the three statements above that will give the scientists the answer?

Regarding statement 1: They have no idea. I'm afraid it's back to the drawing board - and the technical designer. He will give you an idea!

Regarding statement 2: The scientists say the vast ring is mysterious. There is no mystery within a mind that is eternal and continuously creative.

Regarding statement 3: The scientists say the vast ring (or enormous Halo) contradicts all current models of the universe. God is Symmetry, Order and Perfect Design. There is no contradiction within Divinity. That's why the reasoning of the scientists is wrong. They cannot fathom out an equation that puts order in the FIRST PLACE.

CHAPTER 35

Other Stars

1 Main Sequence star

2 T Tauri-Star or Herbigae/Be Star

3 ProtoStar

4 Super Giant star

5 Variable stars

6 Runaway stars

7 Hypervelocity stars.

8 Intergalactic stars

9 White Dwarfs

10 Stephenson 2–18 largest star in the whole cosmos

This further list of stars is not exhaustive.

The complexity of the galaxies is shown within this list of stars. The enormous variety and varying origins of these stars lean towards a specific and intelligent source.

My mind cannot comprehend the infinite number of examples of time and space, within our very specially designed cosmos.

Each new day, scientists come across more complex problems.

Solving the problems IS THE PROBLEM.

CHAPTER 36

Why Stars Twinkle

Stars are so far away they appear as pinpoints of light in the night sky.

Since all light comes from a single point (origin) the path is very sensitive to atmospheric interference.

When the light passes through the atmosphere, it is bent countless times due to refraction, making it look as though the stars are blinking.

The sun doesn't twinkle because it is too close to Earth, compared to the other stars.

The true source of all light is contained in my theory of "The Order of Creation."

Now, scientists are saying they have detected light <u>before,</u> as they call it, "the Big Bang," which is truly the Baptism and envelopment of all creation.

Light comes from ONE Source – Intelligent Design.

Have scientists grasped the Eternal Force of Light?

Space time will tell.

CHAPTER 37

Phonetic Sounds

As we move methodically through this book, we have studied the content and amazing structures of the heavens.

We have also looked at the sounds emitted from the earth and planet.

Although we have touched on a number of celestial bodies, I would still like to examine further areas of the cosmos, for instance, meteors and comets, but that's for later.

Let us look at a more down-to-earth and human aspect.

Speech patterns in humans is an interesting and varied topic to investigate.

The human voice consists of sound made by a human being using the vocal tract, such as talking, singing, laughing, crying, screaming, shouting and yelling etc. The human voice frequency is specifically a part of human sound production in which the vocal folds (vocal cords) are the primary sound source (other than the feeding mechanics and connections to the brain).

Other sound production mechanisms produced from the same general area of the body involve the production of unvoiced consonants, clicks, whistling and whispering.

Generally speaking, the mechanism for generating the human voice can be sub-divided into three parts: the lungs, the vocal folds within the larynx (voice box) and the articulators.

The lungs (the "pump") must produce adequate airflow and air pressure to vibrate the vocal folds. The vocal folds (vocal cords) then vibrate to use airflow from the lungs to create audible <u>pulses</u> (see previous reference to <u>Pulsar</u>) that form the laryngeal sound source.

The muscles of the larynx adjust the length and tension of the vocal folds to "fine tune" – pitch and tone. The articulators, the part of the vocal tract above the larynx coexisting of tongue, palate, cheek and lips etc, articulate and filter the sound emanating from the larynx and to some degree can interact with the laryngeal airflow to strengthen or weaken it as a sound source.

The vocal folds in combination with the articulators (and brain signals) are capable of producing highly intricate arrays of sound. TIF tone of voice may be modulated to suggest emotion, such as anger, surprise, fear, happiness, or sadness.

The human voice is used to express emotions, and can also reveal the age and sex of the speaker (and the word became flesh and dwelt among us).

Singers use the human voice as an instrument for creating music.

Ref -Wikipedia.

Can the spoken word be inspired by thoughts?

It seems logical to assume that before any word is spoken phonetically, it is really a thought transfer (pre-birth).

This thought is transmitted from the brain as a signal to form (formation) our words.

When the <u>formation</u> is ready, the phonetic sound takes over and produces the <u>birth</u> of conversation and language.

The molecular structure of a spoken word is totally dependent on the systematic signal that is received from the brain.

114

Does every word we speak have a different molecular structure?

Yes must be the answer, for every word we speak is more or less different.

Of course, certain words will be repeated in conversation but this constant - is entirely dependent on the readjustment of the brain signal (instantaneously). So the molecular structure of the varying spoken words will be different, merely because the phonetic sound of each word has a differential – inbuilt within the utterance. Every thought we have in our brain can be easily transferred by a signal to the vocal cord, resulting in varying conversational differences.

For instance, if we have a violent thought, this can be transferred to our speaking voice, which can result in an angry phonetic word that can quite often lead to violent behaviour.

Similarly, if we have good thoughts, this signal of goodness can result in a loving formation of pulses, which generate tender phonetic words.

A spectrogram of the human voice showing its rich harmonic content, is almost skeletal - like the human bone structure. (see spectrogram)

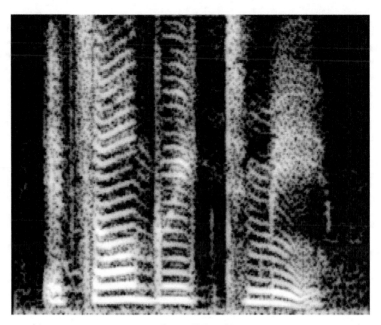

Therefore, it seems that the molecules in the actual spoken word will change according to mood and the environment.

If anger is present in our mind, the molecular structure in the spoken word will be tense, causing a stress to the actual formation of cellular solidification. In other words, the five molecules within the actual phonetic angry word will be erratic, causing a reverberation back to the brain, which quite often will increase the mode of anger.

Regarding the relativity of the human spoken word and the eternal words of creation, when Moses received the Ten Commandments, he asked God, "What is your name?

The answer from God was, "I Am Who I Am" (like the fire that transforms everything to itself).

This phonetic sound came from the Inventor of Words.

I previously spoke about the birth process of a thought in humans.

But we have to realise God's thoughts and ways are NOT our ways.

Therefore, there was no pre-birth of a thought within the supernatural structure of intelligent design.

The process of thought was intelligently designed by God in the first place and was ALWAYS there anyway.

So, God's processes of thought, word and deed are infinite.

God appeared to Moses as a Burning Bushfire (see image of the Sun).

Fire burns; fire brings heat; fire is the Holy Spirit of Creation and the cosmos.

The Word can become flesh in you. If you will receive the Word in your spirit, it will manifest in your flesh and in the material world where our bodies exist. The promises of God will be turned into facts in your bones, muscles, organs, brain, and tissues in your body, and in your spoken word.

The Word will drive out depression and hopelessness that has locked itself in your tissues as you renew your mind to the words of Jesus. The Word is to be written in our flesh for all to read, for Psalm 42:11 says that He is the "health of our countenance." When people look upon us, they should see Jesus the Word manifest in our flesh. For we are now His Body and His representatives upon the earth.

In conclusion to this chapter on "Phonetic Sounds," we can see correlations and connections to the promises of God. The countenance within our human body structure will resonate and be even more receptive to the fire of creation in the galaxies – when mankind truly accepts the supernatural grace and Baptism of creation.

CHAPTER 38

Balance and Poise

The Supernatural Grace and Baptism of Creation must involve some form of Balance and Poise.

First of all, let us try to look at the *noun meaning*.

The difference between balance and poise is that balance is (uncountable) - it is a state in which opposing forms Harmonise equilibrium – while poise (obsolete) weight; an amount of weight – the amount something weighs.

As a *verb meaning*:

The difference between balance and poise is that balance is to make (items) weigh up while poise is (obsolete) to hang in equilibrium – to be balanced or suspended.

Balance is one of my favourite words in the English language.

To keep the balance in everything that we do or say is a wonderful attribute in life.

To weigh-up situations.

The Order of Creation would have been nothing without

balance and poise.

Any opposing molecular forms (matter) would have been instantly harmonised through the Supernatural and Eternal Reasoning: judgement and poise of the Creator.

Poise is equilibrium and balance.

The poise of Creation is almost like the graceful movements of a ballet dancer – seemingly effortless and full of harmony.

The symphony of operatic music is a sweet sound to the ears of the ballet dancer, and she responds in graceful flowing movement that seems to cut through the atmosphere with an elegance that is <u>flowing and creative</u>.

This analogy of the ballet dancer's movements explains fully the eternal reasoning of God.

CHAPTER 39

Dexterity and Finesse

Throughout the vast realm of nothingness - at the moment of formation and baptism of the universes - was there within the formless void, a series of intelligent pulses that mobilised the birth process into a sublime order?

For instance, envelopment and supernatural grace are within themselves guided, like the fire that transforms everything into itself.

Are we to assume and theorise that some form of Intelligence was actually within the void of nothingness at its conception and formation?

If that is so, we can certainly say, "nothing comes from nothing."

Therefore, a baptismal formation would easily inherit a form of dexterity and finesse.

If a formless void just happens to "happen," what reasoning is contained within "the happening"?

Is it also safe to say that dexterity and finesse would also be missing within the lack of reasoning and continuity of form.

Assumption can be a dangerous tool to use. It covers up the cracks of uncertainty and vagueness!

However, if the *assumption* is based on a reasonably sound "order of progression," then the *if* factor is removed and replaced with an "intuitive knowing" about the reasons for creation.

If God so wished, he would allow dexterity and finesse to automatically filter through the baptismal process, which in turn would glorify and adorn the sublime array of Cosmic gifts.

A gift, when received, is normally the reason for the receiver to be prompted into a mode of genuine happiness and thanksgiving.

If there is no gift given (weddings and birthdays etc) there is normally a feeling of surprise and sadness.

The finesse of a loving gesture is sprinkled with a certain dexterity of thought and action, which leads to the reason for giving in the first place.

Knowing knowledge is present when the person who receives the gift appreciates this fine charitable gesture and reciprocates with an affectionate hug or smile.

If a happening (no reason) just happens, the recipient is normally confused and bewildered.

Therefore, sequential Form and Baptism lead to order, which in turn brings to the recipient's awareness and receptivity.

If we look at the descriptive meaning of dexterity, it means "mental skill or quickness" – an apt description of what was involved in the Baptism of the universes and galaxies.

Aligned to dexterity is finesse, which is a synonym for dexterity in the area of skill topics.

In some cases, you can use "finesse" instead of the noun "dexterity" when it comes to subjects such as deftness, aptitude, or even smartness.

The descriptive meaning of finesse means great skill or style, in being able to deal with a situation in a skilful manner.

Did intelligent design look *to form* dexterity and finesse?

Of course not. Dexterity and finesse were already inherent in the design manufacture.

The ability to perform a difficult action quickly and skilfully with the <u>hands</u>! This further description of Dexterity gives a little hint to a loving Creator who formed everything with a gentle caress of his loving hands.

We can even have vocal dexterity, which means the ability to deliver difficult and complicated talks or sermons with apparent ease.

In earlier chapters, I spoke about the sound waves from pulsars and planets.

Intelligent design has great vocal dexterity in communicating Love to the planet earth; are we listening?

CHAPTER 40

Catch a Falling Comet

I mentioned earlier that I would speak about comets and meteors (see previous photograph)

In March 2020, a space telescope located another comet called "Neowise." The comet was named after the telescope that first spotted it.

This particular comet is currently millions of miles from Earth, and during its closest approach on July 23rd, 2020, it will still be 64 million miles off - or about 400 times further away than the moon.

Nasa said the comet was "putting on a spectacular night-time display."

It added: "It made its once-in-our-lifetimes close approach to the sun on July 3rd, 2020 and will cross outside Earth's orbit on its way back to the outer parts of the solar system by mid-August."

A comet is made of gas dust (dust to dust), ice and rock, tending to come from the furthest regions of our solar system and move in long orbits.

Here we have <u>dust</u> being mentioned again – same as the chapter about (nebula).

How are comets formed?

Comets are small, icy objects that circle the sun. They can be thought of as floating time capsules, preserving a chemical record of the early solar system.

Astronomers believe comets materialized more than 4.5 billion years ago from the <u>dust</u> and gas of the protoplanetary disk, a donut-shaped cloud of debris surrounding our newborn star. On the fringes of the disk, far from the sun's heat, fine grains of dust coated with frozen gases and water ice began clumping (Intelligent formation and origin) together.

Over time, clumps of dust assembled into ice-rich rocks, which later transformed into the mile-sized bodies that we observe today travelling among and far beyond the planets. *Ref Nasa Vis*

Time and time again, we see the involvement of DUST.

"And unto dust, you shall return" (returning orbit).

Is this just a coincidence that a comet is made up partly of dust?

Did it just happen?

Or is there something else at work?

Once again, I will leave you to discern and decide.

Ref: American Meteor Society-Meteor Activity Outlook - July 9th- 15th 2016.

CHAPTER 41

Meteor

A meteor is a small body of matter from outer space that enters the Earth's atmosphere, becoming incandescent as a result of friction and appearing as a streak of light.

Meteors can be detected by the sounds they give off as they pass through the atmosphere. They are sometimes known as shooting stars – but in reality, they are not stars.

Once again, we see a celestial body emitting sound waves.

I covered this topic of celestial body sounds previously. Again, this leads us to the theory of origin, reasoning, and the formation of vocal dexterity.

There are also meteoroids, which are small, rocky or metallic bodies in outer space.

Meteoroids are significantly smaller than asteroids and range in size from (small grains, as a mustard seed) to one-metre-wide objects.

Objects smaller than this are classed as micrometeoroids or space dust (dust again).

Most are fragments from comets or asteroids, whereas others are collision impact debris ejected from bodies such as the Moon or Mars.

Dust particles everywhere, remnants of origin and creation. Comets, asteroids, meteors, meteoroids, and micrometeoroids - they all LINK together, similar to my bicycle chain theory.

CHAPTER 42

Dark Matter

Hidden within all forms of celestial activity is dark matter.

Dark matter is non-luminous material that is postulated to exist in space. It could take any of several forms, including weakly interacting particles (dark matter) or high energy randomly moving particles created after the Baptism of the galaxies.

Therefore, the envelopment of the whole cosmos - through supernatural Baptism - spread a series of randomly moving particles throughout the universe, which is still evident today.

Dark matter is thought to account for 85% of the matter in the universe.

Linking up with dark matter is dark energy, which consists of 73% of the total mass in the universe.

It is called dark matter because it does not appear to interact with the electromagnetic field – which means it doesn't absorb, reflect, or emit electromagnetic radiation and is, therefore, difficult to detect.

Dark matter is a complete mystery, but scientists say that it is an important mystery!

The Swiss astronomer Fritz Zwicky first used the term "dark matter" in the 1930s.

It is still one of the great mysteries of science. They are studying dark matter by using gravitational lensing.

Throughout the thesis of this book, I have tried to show methodically and directly the reasoning behind my answers - to refute and unravel the "Big Bang" theory.

If you are an outsider looking in at my theories, I sincerely hope you can discern my logic, and, hopefully, try to fathom out why I am totally for intelligent design and a supernatural creator, who just happens to be called God Almighty.

I think I have put forward powerful arguments to try to sway any doubters.

If, at the end of the day, there is no sway towards intelligent design, then that's okay too. We live in a democracy, and everyone is entitled to their opinion.

Let us get back to dark matter.

As you can see from the scientists' theories, they are baffled by dark matter! Can a creator even allow alternative forces?

They say it's a complete mystery because it does not appear to interact with the electromagnetic field – which means it doesn't absorb, reflect, or emit electromagnetic radiation and is, therefore, difficult to detect.

You don't say!

Formation – intelligent formation, that is –has a very clever card trick up its sleeve – you're not meant to unravel these mysteries too easily! I have demonstrated throughout my book the complexities that Science brings to the drawing board. But, as I have said previously, if we go to the designer of the blueprint for dark mass, it's not a problem for _Him_ (gender male – procreation!)

Dark matter, therefore, is implied in a variety of astrophysical observations, including gravitational effects that cannot be explained by accepted theories of gravity unless more matter is present than can be seen.

For this reason, most experts think that dark matter is abundant in the universe and that it has had a strong influence on its structure and formation.

If dark matter is abundant in the universe, and is a mystery, can we safely theorise that an omnipotent force put it there? Here is an interesting analogy: this same omnipotent force allowed Lucifer to rebel, knowing full well that Lucifer would be banished from Heaven because of the inherent, unfathomable, and sovereign justice of God.

Would that solve the mystery?

If you are a believer, it's an easy answer.

If you are an atheist, it tends to be an unusual answer, to say the least!

Again, part of the solving of the origins of dark matter depends on supernatural grace, taking into account that God allowed Lucifer to spawn darkness.

Whosoever believes in supernatural grace is already on the starting blocks and finds creation an easy fact to understand. If you don't believe in, or even accept supernatural grace, therein lies the problem.

This statement is not said with any degree of take-it-or-leave-it-attitude, but my mind at this moment goes out to anyone who is against the fact of supernatural grace.

I genuinely offer my hand of love and friendship in the hope that we can at least agree to disagree.

With this in mind, I think it is pertinent to include details about atheism.

CHAPTER 43

Atomic Whirl

The atomic whirl is the logo of the American atheists and has come to be used as a symbol of atheism in general, as some American atheist members claim.

(Unfortunately, the logo is under copyright).

The atomic whirl is based on the Rutherford model of the atom, which has been proven wrong, erroneously showing the orbital paths of electrons around the central nucleus and not on the atomic orbitals, which is the near-perfect experimental approximation.

The logo resembles the logos and symbols of the US Atomic Energy Authority Commission and the International Atomic Energy Agency, which also based their designs on the erroneous Rutherford Model.

The symbol is used by the American Atheist Organization to symbolise that "only through the use of scientific analysis and free open enquiry can humankind reach out for a better life."

The lower part of the central loop is left open, or "broken," to represent the fact that atheists accept that, while they rely on the scientific method, they are, in essence, searching for the answers, and in some cases, further questions. The central loop of the logo forms an "A" which represents the atheists. *Ref Wikipedia*

In explaining atomic structure a little further, much of an atom's positive charge is concentrated in a relatively tiny volume at the centre of the atom, known today as the nucleus.

The meaning of nucleus: (noun) The central and most important part of an object (universe) movement or group is the fundamental basis for its activity and growth.

Physics: The positively charged central core of an atom, consisting of protons and neutrons, contains nearly all of its mass.

Biology: A dense organelle present in most eukaryotic cells, typically a single rounded structure bounded by a double membrane containing the genetic material.

Anatomy: A discreet mass of grey matter in the central nervous system.

I would like now to try to explain atheism in a broader sense, but before I do, here are my further comments about the atheist logo.

I think, first of all, it is extremely honest of the atheist society to admit they are continuing to search for the answers, whilst adding their questions to a quest that, to be honest, will never end.

When I notice the "broken" part of the logo, it raises the question of; where is the final formation and closure of their theories? Brokenness is a symptom of the world's problems at the moment.

The opposite of the brokenness is a completely symmetrical and never-ending symbol 8.

I am trying to be as objective as I can about the theories of atheism, but when the atheists themselves tell us that they are always "searching for the answers," that honesty becomes lost within the wealth of supernatural evidence

Atheism is an absence of belief in the existence of deities (God Almighty).

It is a rejection of the belief that any deities exist.

Atheism is contrasted with theism, which in its general form, is the belief that at least one deity exists.

The word atheism originated before the 5th century BC, and its meaning is from the Greek (*athios*), meaning, "without gods."

During the 16th century, the word atheism emerged after the spread of sceptical enquiry and a subsequent increase in criticism of religion.

During the 18th century, the "Age of Enlightenment" spread throughout France, resulting in the French Revolution, which was noted for its "unprecedented atheism."

This revolution was the first major political movement in history to advocate for the supremacy of human reason.

In 2011, 61% of people in China reported they were atheists.

During a Eurobarometer survey in 2010, the European Union (EU) reported that 20% of the EU population claimed not to believe in "any sort of spirit, God or life force," with France (40%) and Sweden (34%) representing the highest totals.

CHAPTER 44

Pleasure

Did God create the whole of the cosmos because it pleased him and gave him pleasure?

I believe it was done with that very reasoning; his in-built supernatural and creative intelligence ensured the maximum delight and fruition of his wonderful planning for mankind and the whole of Creation.

God is Love. Therefore, Love is eternal.

When the void of space existed in infinity, Love was there resting meekly.

When the Father in Heaven decided to create the cosmos, his mind was already "in love" with his concept of the human race.

His mind, being all-powerful, gave each individual human being freedom of will.

How wonderful is that gift, for if we did not have "freedom of will," we would be robots.

Unfortunately, because of the pure intention of Love, other negative forces (positive and negative poles repel) using the "freedom of will" gift, decided to rebel against God because of pride. Pride prompted some celestial angels to try to fight against goodness.

Lucifer was the leader of the rebellious angels.

Love conquered the pride-filled angels through the great leadership of St Michael the Archangel.

Therefore, the formation of the planetary systems (although formed out of love) became sprinkled with dissent, especially within the hierarchy of angels and eventually the human race.

Today we are seeing this dissent proliferate to such an extent that it almost seems that the proliferation could well result in total anarchy.

So, Love in itself is fragile.

There's a saying, Love conquers all.

Love, in its openness, can leave us vulnerable to emotional and violent oppression.

God, being Love, knows all of this. He already knew what was to happen. Why, then, did he create everything?

Because He wanted to.

His everlasting and infinite mind, through subtlety, dexterity, reasoning and pleasure, is always in control.

We just have to look at the planetary systems to see how these systems move in seemingly graceful orbits.

Galaxies mix with other galaxies.

I am sure the whole vastness of the cosmos gives great pleasure to the scientists.

New "surprises" are being discovered every day. Nothing seems to stay still.

"Always" is proof of divine intelligence.

The complexities of the universes were put there in the first place by a mind that is not complex.

It's just that we humans find the wonders of the Heavens complex!

We only have to look at dark matter again.

Scientists are completely baffled by this original thought of God. His thoughts are not our thoughts.

Will the Earth as it is end up destroying itself by human greed, lust for power, and nuclear war?

Only God knows.

He may well become angry at the continual abuse of his loving gifts, gifts that we are meant to accept and enjoy.

For instance, the gift of sexual intercourse and human orgasm.

Isn't God wonderful? Not only does He give us the fantastic design of the human body, He also gives us pleasure within the human orgasm to procreate.

Human beings sometimes accept gifts (as I said earlier), or they reject gifts.

The gift of sexual intercourse has been abused for centuries. Pornography is rampant, and sexual child abuse is a horror that cannot even be contemplated.

Are we to change and accept the gift of Love from God, or do we carry on with a selfish and ignorantly blissful existence, continually staining the mosaic of creation?

There WILL be an ending.

There WILL be a judgement.

Because the Sovereignty of the Creator will automatically (without thinking) bring our own actions into sharp focus in a sort of "Illumination of Conscience."

Then, and only then, we will be made aware of the futility of war, vengeance, and hatred.

Love, it seems, will unravel everything, just like Einstein when he "discovered" the theory of relativity.

My eureka moment during the writing of this book was realising that *I was actually writing it!*

I have strayed into a specialised domain of thinking.

I, by the grace of God alone, have put forward theories as to "The Order of Creation."

Creative forces touched my mind in an invigorating way.

Whether scientists look at my theories with disdain, shock or disbelief I, an engineer, within myself, feel content in the knowledge that to have written and produced my theory of creation there could only have been one answer to it: divine inspiration.

At present, the whole world needs to sit up and take notice.

Worldwide events seem to be spinning out of control.

Only the human soul cannot be harmed.

They can take my body, but my soul remains intact because, at the moment of creation, it was already there within me.

These words are the scientist "within me."

I cannot change society, *unless I change myself first.*

Have I "changed" during the writing of this book?

I have certainly realised in a more detailed way the complexities of the cosmos.

If an atheist was writing this book, would there be a "leaning" towards the big bang philosophy? I would hazard a guess and say yes.

However, the human mind is very complex.

So, why are their believers and non-believers about God and intelligent design?

Is there a supernatural element to the belief system?

In my work as a Christian evangelist and a retired engineer, I have witnessed some extraordinary manifestations of the human body.

I have assisted at real-life exorcisms where I came face to face with the reality of demons.

In fact, there is a fairly well-known story about psychiatrist Scott J Peck who at the time was an atheist.

He asked to be present at an exorcism being conducted by a Catholic priest.

He witnessed the person who was being exorcised take on a visible and reptilian form of a snake.

This incident made Scott Peck a believer.

He knew in his heart that the human mind could not produce this truly physical manifestation of evil.

Some exorcisms involve actual physical levitation during the Exorcism Rite, performed by the demon within the person being exorcised.

Now I know some atheistic scientists may well pour scorn on these very real and often disturbing events.

But why pour scorn? Is it a reluctance to discover "The Truth?"

One favourite "trick" of Satan (he does exist, just ask Satanists!) is to whisper into the ear of non-believers, "that he doesn't exist."

So the whole realm of the supernatural, which I have touched on occasionally within my book, does exist.

Just read Scott Peck's book *The People of the Lie,* and you will truly begin to see the very real existence of the supernatural realm.

I am convinced that induced ignorance has a big part to play in the reluctance to explore the Intelligent Design Theory.

Further to induced ignorance is the very real fact that sometimes people, no matter what the proof is, just don't want to change! It's true. It's a leave-me-to-myself attitude!

And, of course, these comments can apply to believers who try to pour scorn on atheists too.

Moving on, there also seems to be a reluctance by atheists and atheistic scientists to explore the very real world of the supernatural (which I have described through my experiences of the Exorcism Rite).

Avoidance of these particular subjects can sometimes be induced by a subtle prompting from the unseen forces of evil.

This, in turn, leads to a sort of "ignorance is bliss attitude." Or, "what I switch off from" really doesn't exist.

Take it from me, the realities of the supernatural world, and in particular, exorcisms, are very real. I have already stated that I have been involved in the supernatural realm of Exorcisms. I have witnessed first-hand the destructiveness of demonic powers.

This particular witnessing of my evangelistic work is also written in another of my books titled *You Are Mine Now,* which can be ordered through Amazon or at my website: www.foundationoftruth.org.uk

Throughout the writings within this book, I have always tried to give the "flip side" to both arguments for – and against God.

I hope that through my reasonably methodical approach, people who read this book will at least feel a sense of "let us look at this differently" approach.

I hope you, the readers, have found areas of *Into the Mind of Infinity* enlightening.

In writing this book, I was taken on a journey that really "blew my mind."

The Infinite Creator God Almighty took my hand and placed His loving hand in mine, creating this book.

I am not a scientist, but through divine inspiration, I think a reasonable hypothesis for intelligent design has been demonstrated and produced.

If we have the gift of revelation there is an <u>Order</u> of knowledge (see Order Of Creation) that we cannot arrive at by our own powers but is granted to us by the Holy Spirit.

If we are truly open to the Holy Spirit's work in our lives, by God's grace, we can receive fresh insight into the meaning of origin and the cosmos.

St Thomas Aquinas taught: "Knowledge gained in this way is more certain than knowledge gained through reason, the certainty that the divine light gives is greater than that which the light of natural reason gives."

Finally, when all is said and done, we, the population of God's good Earth, are truly NOT important.

A hermit once wrote, "One who knows does not say."

And "one who says does not know."

Ending with these words from Socrates seems appropriate: "The only true wisdom is in knowing – that you know nothing."

In my opinion, Science and Religion are becoming closer in many different ways.

It is good to question.

This book has put questions and unique theories together, showing that it is all right to agree to disagree.

I only hope that the questions posed by both Religion and Science will ultimately lead to a greater cohesion of minds and beliefs, resulting in a better world for all of us.

Scientific Fact

Most FRBS (Fast Radio Bursts) which are strong bursts of radio waves , from galaxies billions of light years away last just a few milliseconds before blinking out and are one off events.

Recently, a new signal or radio wave from deep space has been discovered. This new signal - FRB20191221A lasts up to three seconds, making it 1000 times longer than the average FRB, and also has the clearest repeated pattern discovered so far.

"It was unusual," researcher Daniele Michilli of The Massachusetts Institute of Technology's (MIT) Kavli Institute for Astrophysics and Space Research said in a statement, "Not only was it very lasting about three seconds, but there were periodic peaks that were remarkably precise, emitting every fraction of a second - boom boom boom, - *LIKE A HEARTBEAT.*"

The End

ACKNOWLEDGEMENTS

I thank all contributors to the sections on Astronomy, DNA and Cosmology etc, and, where possible, I have referenced important back-up information from different sources, including Professor of Mathematics John D Barrow of Cambridge University.

Further grateful thanks go to John Smith (Scientist BSC, C Chem) for his valuable comments Foreword and Critique, and last but not least to my friend and Editor, Matthew Lynch, former Production Editor and Chief Sub Editor, *The Sunday Times*.

With love to everyone.

Email: joelivingston1967@gmail.com

REFERENCES

Page 7- Chapter 1.Always Is. E=MC2 Albert Einstein

Page 12 - Chapter 3. Cause and Effect. St Thomas Aquinas (5 ways to Prove That God Exists)

Page 16- Chapter 4. Infinity. Cosmological Infinities . (Professor John D Barrow, Prof ' of Mathematics at Cambridge University- Overseer of E Magazine +

Page 31 Chapter 7.D.N.A. - D.N.A. Structure.Com

Page 32 Chapter 8. D.N.A. - Molecule – D.N.A. Structure .Com- Can Eternal Love be Seen Under a Microscope

Page 35 Chapter 10. Splitting The Atom - lanl.gov/history/atomicbchb/trinity/shtml

Page 37 Chapter 11.When We See A Chair Is It Actually A Chair? https//link.springer.com/chapteric1007/978-3-662-09291-03

Page 43 Chapter 13.Theory Of Relativity Albert Einstein – General Relativity 1915-Special Relativity 1905-simple Wikipedia.

Page 46 Chapter 14.Metamorphosis – Tadpole Galaxy- www.haaretz.com/science-health/magazine

Page 55 Chapter 16. Making Form Out Of The Formless, Gen 1 v1-31- big bangwiki+pedia.org/wiki/big_bang

Page 60 Chapter 18. Living Organism – Anton Shkaplerov 2017 Tass + – Quora.

Page 69-70 Chapter 21.Nebula (noun) www.differencebetween.net/science/difference-betweennebula-and-galaxy/#1xzz6q02

Page 73 Chapter 22. What Is The Eternal Soul- School Of Apologetics (CCC 362)

Page 78 Chapter 23. Galaxy Types and Sizes - www.doesgodexist.org/novdec01/isaacnewtonandgods

Printed in Great Britain
by Amazon

16416358R00088